# JOBS IN
# TRAVEL
# AND TOURISM

# JOBS IN
# TRAVEL
# AND TOURISM

Christine Swanson

*SECOND EDITION*

KOGAN
PAGE

## Acknowledgements

*The author would like to thank the following for their kind assistance: Bradford Metropolitan Council; J Morris Bray (for photographs on pages 24, 45, 49 and 50); British Caledonian Airways; Cornish Traditional Cottages; D C Cook; English Tourist Board; Falcon Sailing; Intasun; James Hill Travel; Kirklees Metropolitan Council; Townsend Thoresen; Woodcock Travel; Yorkshire and Humberside Tourist Board.*

First published in Great Britain in 1985 by
Kogan Page Limited
120 Pentonville Road, London N1 9JN
Second edition 1988
Copyright © Kogan Page Ltd 1985, 1988

**British Library Cataloguing in Publication Data**
Swanson, Christine
    Jobs in travel and tourism — 2nd ed.
    1. Tourist trade — Vocational guidance —
    Great Britain
    I. Title
    338.4'79141'0023     G155.5
    ISBN 1-85091-541-5

Typeset by DP Photosetting, Aylesbury, Bucks
Printed and bound in Great Britain by
The Camelot Press Ltd, Southampton

# Contents

# Introduction

Travel and tourism is one of the largest and most quickly developing industries in the United Kingdom today. On the holiday side, as people gain more leisure time, they are tending to take more than one holiday a year, often having short breaks away from home in between as well. At the same time, as travel by air, sea, road and rail becomes quicker and cheaper, business travellers think no more about commuting to meetings abroad than they do about travelling from London to Glasgow. The world is shrinking fast!

This book gives you an insight into the wide range of jobs which involve assisting tourists and independent and business travellers.

Part 1 looks at jobs at home or abroad with tour operators, the main transport providers, travel agencies, and with those organisations who have the task of developing tourism at home. Some of the people who are doing such work describe their day-to-day activities, giving you a chance to compare the glamorous images of some of their jobs with the reality.

Part 2 gives suggestions on how to get into the industry, and describes what training is available, what sort of courses can be taken, how experience can be gained, and where to find further help and information.

# Part 1

## Chapter 1

# Tour Operators: How Holidays are Arranged

This chapter, and the next two, look at the 'holiday' side of the travel industry. There are many different kinds of operator who arrange holiday packages, whether they are for incoming tourists from abroad, outgoing visitors from Britain, or stay-at-home holiday-makers going to other parts of the country. There are large companies like Thomson, Cosmos, Thomas Cook, Intasun and others, who provide a wide range of holidays and give supplies of their brochures to travel agents, who then do the job of actually selling the holidays to customers over the counter. The travel agent receives a commission from the tour operator, usually of around 10 per cent for each holiday sold in this way. Then there are much smaller companies, some of whom sell direct to their customers, without using a travel agent. The idea of direct selling is to keep costs down; 'direct sell' companies are often small, and in many cases specialise in one type of holiday.

The typical package tour consists of many different components, including the travel, the accommodation (which could be a hotel, campsite or self-catering apartment), organised excursions and meals. All these parts of the package are put together by the tour operator and sold to the customer. Before looking at the jobs which can be done with tour-operating companies, it is worth seeing *how* these package tours are put together, marketed and finally sold to the customer.

## Putting Together a Package

Even a simple two-week holiday in Spain involves a great deal of work. First of all the resort including its hotels, excursion possibilities, beaches, swimming pools and other facilities have to be checked. When a decision is made to use a particular place as a holiday destination, agreements have to be made and contracts drawn up and signed with the hotel owners, local coach operators, airline companies and others, to make sure that the holiday-makers will find everything satisfactory once they arrive.

All this 'research and planning' is carried out by people who have already had a great deal of experience in the industry. They need this as the planning is done many months before the holiday-makers are actually on their way; a successful tour operator has to be able to predict what the travelling public will want well in advance.

## Selling the Packages

Once a package holiday has been put together, and all the different parts assembled, it has to be presented to the customers. This is achieved through making up attractive and colourful brochures, usually containing a write-up about each resort, with photographs of hotels and other attractions. Brochures are advertised in newspapers, magazines, on television, and are given in bulk to travel agencies for them to display. Direct sell companies who do not use travel agencies advertise in a similar way, but may also use special interest publications, such as camping magazines for camping holidays, or skiing magazines for skiing holidays.

Many tour operators have a close relationship with the different travel agents, and some have their own travel agency outlets too. Apart from providing the agents with brochures, tour operators arrange 'promotions' to familiarise the agents with the holidays on offer. These are quite often social events, such as an evening spent at a

hotel or conference centre where a representative may show a video, describe some of the facilities on offer and answer questions about the holidays. Tour operators selling through travel agents also employ sales representatives, who spend most of their time 'on the road' travelling around to visit the different travel agents and encouraging them to sell their firm's holidays.

## Buying a Holiday

Buying a holiday is not very different from buying anything else in a shop; many people go into a travel agency, choose from one of the brochures and make a booking. The clerk then places the booking for them by telephoning the tour operator with all the details of the customer and his/her requirements. With direct selling companies, the customers make their own telephone booking.

In both cases the telephone bookings are usually provisional to begin with, so that the customer has a day or two to fill in a booking form and post it off with a deposit to make it a firm purchase. Travel agents help their customers to complete these forms, and advise on insurance, medical requirements, visas and passports. Most companies also send out an invoice, asking for full payment about eight to ten weeks before departure. There are many occasions when a holiday-maker only decides to take a holiday at short notice, so the whole process is speeded up and full payment may have to be made immediately if the booking is made within six weeks of departure.

## The Structure of a Tour Operator's Office

One of the larger tour-operating companies selling holidays through travel agencies is Intasun. The research, planning, brochure production and advertising are organised from their head office in Bromley.

◀ *A busy small tour operator's office*

The company has a number of regional offices, one of which is in Bradford. Over 250 people work in this branch, which sells around 400,000 holidays a year through travel agencies all over Britain. Like all offices there are several different departments at Intasun, including reservations for taking bookings; customer services, which deals with queries and any complaints; accounts; a despatch department which sends out information from the computer; and the computer centre which serves all the group's offices from this one installation. Like many tour operators Intasun introduced computers into their work a few years ago. This has made the work easier and more accurate, and has also meant that a great deal more work can be done by the same number of people.

While Intasun is one of the larger tour operators, there are many small companies operating in this country. Take Cornish Traditional Cottages for example. This is a small company, specialising in the letting of cottages in Cornwall to customers who come from the UK and abroad. While it started as a family business, there are now eight full-time staff and two part-timers. The staff working in the company take a lot of pride in providing a personal service to guests, to owners of properties and to anyone else they become involved with – the kind of service that the big companies would also like to offer, but find more difficult simply because of their size.

The company has two directors, a secretary, a clerk, a general manager, an accounts clerk, a property manager with a clerical assistant, and the two part-time staff. They now organise the letting of cottages owned by the company, as well as by other people. They charge a commission of 20 per cent for the service they provide, which covers all costs of advertising, brochure production, postage, invoicing, collection of deposits and final payments, and the dispersal of monies to the owners. The owners are kept up to date on all bookings, and the company issues a questionnaire to guests after their holidays, so that they can monitor their service. This also works as an 'early warning system in case of any developing problems'.

## Chapter 2

# Jobs at Home with Tour Operators

While a home-based job in a tour operator's office may not seem as glamorous as work overseas, there is still plenty of responsibility and organisational ability needed in selling holidays, advising customers and then matching their requirements with what is available. The work is busy and the atmosphere lively and there is still the chance to visit resorts and sites, on behalf of your company, to see what they offer.

## Reservations Clerk

Shirley Leese is a reservations clerk for Intasun at their Bradford office. She works with other reservations clerks in a bright open-plan office, and sits at a desk using a visual display unit (VDU) with a keyboard. (Many companies, even the smaller ones, now make full use of computers in their bookings procedures.) While this is office work, she has very little paper on her desk apart from a supply of the company's holiday brochures. She wears a small set of headphones with a mouthpiece for speaking into, rather than using an ordinary telephone; her hands are then free to type information about bookings, which is fed directly into the computer memory. The computer can come up with a list of these 'provisional bookings', and these go to the customer services department to be checked against the booking forms arriving a couple of days later from the travel agent. This process confirms the booking.

Shirley has a special responsibility for the skiing holidays and vacations in America, which she particularly enjoys dealing with. Although her contact with clients is usually indirect, through travel agencies, and most of her work is done on the telephone, it is an aspect of the travel trade that she likes. As with many of her colleagues, Shirley did not come into the work straight from school.

□ I came into this job after I had been working in a travel agency. This vacancy was advertised in the local paper, so I applied. I think that having the experience of travel agency work helped me to get this job – and it is a useful background – but it does mean that I probably tend to give more advice on the phone than I should. It's really our job to get on and sell, and we are encouraged in this by getting bonus payments at certain times of the year, especially when we are working on late bookings. In order to speed things up we don't deal with queries or complaints: they go to the customer services department. The idea is that we should just deal with reservations and not waste time.

## Phone Bookings
Contact over the phone with the public and travel agents forms an important part of the work.

□ We have two types of phone line: the ones that light up red are for late bookings, and the white lines are for normal bookings. There is also a separate line that agents use to ring in and confirm bookings, and the more junior staff start on that one. It's normal company policy to take people on to phone work only when they are over 18, as it helps in dealing with people if you are more mature. We take bookings initially and can cancel or amend them once they've been made. We do also offer a certain amount of advice. We are familiar with the brochures, so we can explain what facilities there are for children for example. When the agents ring through we can tell them what seats are available on the planes, what accommodation is available, whether children's places are free and so on.

You don't need to be able to type to do this job, although it probably helps a bit; a lot of the work involves using the number keys which are grouped to the side of the keyboard.

But you do need a fair amount of common sense and you do need to be very accurate. Most of all you need to like talking to people. We may not be meeting them face to face, but we are dealing with a lot of different people all day long.

## Work on the VDU
Shirley's VDU is connected up to the computer, so that when a booking call comes through she keys in the information that is required. These details could include the customer's name, the holiday code number, the travel agency dealing with the booking, the number of rooms required, and how many children are in the party. The option is booked through the computer, which then issues a statement, and later the final invoice, followed by tickets which are sent out to the travel agent. Lists of clients who are travelling are automatically taken from the computer, and these are given to the representatives.

## Promotions Work
While Shirley does not normally meet her customers, she does sometimes come into contact with local travel agents.

☐ They call in for brochures sometimes, or they come in to meet people in the office. Our company organises promotions every quarter, when the agents are invited along to hear about the latest developments. Apart from keeping up to date by attending these promotions, we also have some in-service training, where we are told which holidays to push for the summer months and which ones not to push. We are told about the special offers and are able to air our own views too.

Another part of our training is the 'educational trips'. On average we do about two a year, usually in the off-season times, in May and November, and the last one I went on was to Malaga. But they're not holidays! You fly around the various hotels and look at the rooms and general accommodation, checking out the dining facilities, swimming pools, local shops – everything! It's very hard work. You are up at the crack of dawn, and you don't get time to lie around on the beaches. You don't even have any free time in the evenings. On the Malaga trip I had only one evening free – we had to join in with everything. And when you get back you have to write up a report on the trip. We then circulate the reports so that other people can find out about the holiday resorts.

## Working Conditions

While the educational trips involve long hours, Shirley's normal office hours are from 9 am to 5.30 pm and one and a quarter hours off for lunch. She goes on to say that, although her job involves sitting down for long hours with some pressure to get on and sell the holidays, the atmosphere in the office is relaxed and she can get up and stretch her legs and get a cup of coffee when she likes.

□ I like the atmosphere here. I enjoy working with a lot of people, and it's a big office so I have a lot of colleagues. I think it's an easier job here than in a travel agency – although we do have to sell, there is less pressure. The travel agents have the customers to deal with face to face and they can be very demanding, so you need a lot of patience to deal with them. However, by the time the agents contact us they've made sure the customers have a good idea of what they want, although sometimes we do get problems when this doesn't happen and the clients haven't a clue what they really want.

## Qualifications Needed

Shirley was expected to have four GCSEs (grades A–C) or equivalent before she could come into this job, but she adds that common sense is also very important. Many tour operators prefer people to be over 18 before they take them on as reservations or booking clerks, and some experience in a travel agency is obviously helpful. They also tend to look favourably at people who have taken a course of training which has involved some study of travel and tourism, such as a Business and Technician Education Council (BTEC) or a Scottish Vocational Education Council (SCOTVEC) qualification with travel and tourism options, or a Certificate of Travel Agency Competence (COTAC), or Certificate in Travel Studies (CTS). There is a newer qualification now available full time at a few colleges which is designed for those who wish to work in tour operating. This is the Certificate of Tour Operating Practice (COTOP). It can also be taken part time while working or on a YTS.

All these qualifications are explained in Part 2.

## Youth Training Scheme (YTS)

While most tour operators prefer reservations or booking clerks to be over 18, many are becoming involved with the Youth Training Scheme, where younger school-leavers are taken on for placements in the firm, and are given training in reservations and booking procedures. At Intasun, for example, 16-year-old Melanie Bean is on a placement – working alongside the reservations clerks – taking calls from travel agents on the 'confirmations' line, as part of her time on the scheme. She explains how she came to be working with a tour operator:

□ My careers officer suggested I try a YTS, although I had originally thought that it was poorly paid and I'd said I wouldn't go on one of those schemes! But I've found that it's a really good thing. I spend some of my time at college, where I'm doing the COTAC course, and I've done a British Airways basic course and others for Sealink and British Rail. Then I've been on a placement with a travel agency, and now with Intasun.

I've learned a lot during the year, and I've got around to lots of different places. I've been on visits to London and to Yeadon Airport, and we are going on a trip to Paris too, which is partly paid for us. There is another trip arranged to Greece, but we have to pay for ourselves on that.

I wasn't asked for any qualifications to come on to the YTS, although I have got seven CSEs. I think the experience I get here will help me to get a job, and I'd certainly recommend it to people leaving school.

## Administration Clerk

Christine Edwards works as an administration clerk with

Cornish Traditional Holidays at their office in Lostwithiel. She has been in her present job for five years.

◻ I mainly deal with telephone enquiries, send out brochures, deal with any queries from clients, make bookings for them, send out their final invoices, advise them on travel arrangements and keep the owners/housekeepers/keyholders up to date with any last-minute bookings. I occasionally visit some of the properties when time allows, which helps when you're advising clients. I also act as postlady and do any other work that's necessary.

While her firm is much smaller than Shirley's, her work has some similarities on the bookings side. Christine is soon to learn how to use the computer which will assist with booking procedures. The main difference with her job is that she deals directly with her clients and is often expected to give detailed help and advice to them: she sells holidays direct to clients, whereas Shirley deals with travel agents.

Christine had previous experience of general office and travel agency work before she moved into this job. She explains that personality counts a lot when dealing with her clients.

◻ You really need to be bright, cheerful and outgoing, and have a sense of humour. You also need to be able to sell by telephone. It's a busy office, and although there are only a few of us here, the office can become noisy at times depending on the season. In the early booking season, January and February, we occasionally do overtime to keep up to date. I enjoy the work, and I especially like talking to people, and handling difficult guests and owners – it's a challenge! And it's really nice when guests, or even owners, show appreciation of our efforts by sending us a note, or sometimes a personal gift.

*Chapter 3*

# Jobs Overseas with Tour Operators

There are many different types of work done overseas by representatives of tour-operating companies. The job titles vary, even though some of the work itself may be similar. Many of the larger tour operators employ couriers to accompany tours which travel to several different places. Other representatives stay in one resort, working from one hotel or campsite during the season. Children's representatives may also be employed to look after and entertain the children during the day and evening. Companies offering sporting holidays, such as skiing, sailing or trekking, may need ski guides in addition to the resort representative; a sailing flotilla leader and an engineer in addition to the 'hostess'; or a trek leader to accompany a walking or climbing tour. These are just some examples. The actual duties undertaken by each of these representatives vary with the type of holiday being offered.

## Qualities Needed

Representatives, or 'reps', are often the only people employed by the tour-operating company who deal face to face with the customer. This means that the image they have is likely to colour the customer's whole impression of the company. Some are expected to wear a uniform, to help keep up a business-like image, although others such as children's reps may wear the company T-shirt. As reps tend to work on their own or sometimes with just one or two other colleagues, and usually a long way from home, most companies prefer to employ people with a mature attitude and some previous experience of working with people.

The representative's personality is therefore often considered to be more important than academic qualifications alone. Many companies do not ask for any examination passes, although they do ask for fluency in English and, in some cases, a relevant foreign language. While resort reps and couriers need a language, it is not always necessary to speak one in order to work abroad. For example, those overseas reps who are employed for specific jobs, such as ski guides, children's reps and sailing flotilla engineers, may find their skills are more important than their ability to speak a foreign language. Most of their work is with English-speaking holiday-makers or another English-speaking rep anyway.

Most companies have a minimum and maximum age range of around 22 to 35 for their representatives, although a few employ trainees aged 18 or 19, to work alongside overseas reps.

## Special Features of the Work

In many cases reps work on a seasonal basis on short-term contracts, either during the summer season or on winter holidays. Some overseas reps are also able to obtain work in the tour operator's company offices at home, in the off-seasons. However, this is not always possible, so overseas reps have to be prepared to find alternative work when their contracts finish for the season. Few people make a permanent career out of being an overseas rep, although many do it for a few seasons to gain experience of the business, improve their foreign language skills, and to take advantage of the opportunity to travel.

The jobs that representatives do often appear to be glamorous and exciting, but it must be remembered that it is the clients who are on holiday, while the rep is doing a job of work, and one that at times can be very demanding.

## Resort/Hotel Representatives

The duties of an overseas resort or hotel representative vary with the company, but usually involve meeting clients at an airport, or at the end of the main coach journey. The holiday-makers – 'clients' as they are usually called – are then transferred on to a local coach and taken to their hotel, self-catering apartment, campsite or other accommodation. It is usual for the reps to arrange a welcoming party for new arrivals, when they give a speech and provide information about the hotel and its facilities, the resort and surrounding area, and describe any excursions which can be booked by the rep. They also advise on shops and restaurants, car hire and anything else that their clients want to know.

Part of their day is usually set aside for being available in an office at the hotel for clients with queries. The types of problem which they may have to deal with are vast, ranging from lost baggage, to coping with sudden illness, insurance claims, booking excursions, and organising social events such as barbecues and discos. The list is endless and depends very much on the demands of clients. Dealing with local people for much of the time, arranging taxis and excursions for example, makes it necessary for resort reps to have a good knowledge of the local language. They also frequently act as interpreters for their clients, especially when things go wrong!

So a resort rep is often on call 24 hours a day, with considerable disruption to his/her social life. This means that there are no set working hours, making it a job that is definitely unsuitable for anyone wanting a regular and settled life. As reps have to be available for their clients, they normally live in the same accommodation, whether it be a hotel, campsite, or on a sailing yacht. Those who work on the latter two may have a longer season than the hotel reps, as there is preparatory work to be done, with the setting up of tents, cleaning and repair work and maintenance of equipment. There may also be the weekly tasks of

*A representative meeting her clients*

filling up gas canisters, checking boat engines and keeping diesel tanks full.

Most reps also have a certain amount of administrative work to complete each week, such as keeping accounts, ordering replacement equipment, reporting problems, faults and losses of baggage. However, the amount of paperwork is usually small compared to the time spent with clients.

'Specialist' reps such as ski guides and children's reps normally have some of the duties of the general overseas reps described here, and may be expected to deputise sometimes. But they also have their own area of work, and often have a particular qualification or some experience which has helped them to obtain a job abroad.

## Children's Representatives

While most reps are expected to be around 22 or more, those people who have a childcare qualification, such as the National Nursery Examination Board's qualification

(NNEB), may be taken on at the lower age of 18. Some companies also have a maximum age limit and prefer their reps to be single. Gillian Dix is a 'kiddie' rep in her early twenties, and having completed one full season in Spain, is spending the winter working in the Intasun office in Bradford helping in the reservations department. But she is now looking forward to her second season abroad. She explains how she came into the business and what her work involves:

☐ I had started off training as a nursery nurse and got my NNEB qualification at college. But then I went into general nursing for three years. By that time I decided that I would like to travel and move about for a while, so I applied to a lot of different tour-operating companies to see whether they had any vacancies. This particular job was advertised in the *Lady* magazine, so I applied and was lucky, although there was a lot of competition for the job. While I had already trained for working with children I still had to have some instruction at head office before going to Spain. This training was mainly concerned with presenting yourself to a group of clients, and explaining to them what your job involved and what you intended to do with the children. So I had to learn to speak in front of groups of up to 100 people, something I never thought I would have to do! We learned how to help the resort reps with the transfers, which involves getting the clients to their hotels, how to use a microphone, and what to tell people about the resort. We also had to learn about insurance and know what we could and couldn't do.

We look after up to 20 children at a time and their ages range from three to twelve. I work with one other kiddie rep, and we organise all sorts of activities during the day, including playgroups, visits to the beach, sandcastle-building competitions, an evening story time, disco parties with pop and crisps! We also offer a baby patrolling service at night, which is free up to midnight, after which time the client has to pay us a fixed rate. So although we don't work set hours, we usually have some time off during each day, and I work six days a week. My contract was for six months through the summer last year and I really enjoyed it, although I was glad to come home at the end of the season.

Like the hotel reps we are based at the same hotel as the clients, and I shared a room with the other kiddie rep. It means that you don't have much privacy and you have to get on with other people. The social life is very good, although you should be the kind of person who enjoys joining in. It's a very responsible job, especially when you're dealing with children of different ages. Even getting them along the roads and keeping them on the pavements requires constant supervision.

While I enjoy the work I should eventually like to be a resort rep, where I would deal with a wider range of people, including adults. To do that I shall need to be able to speak the language – I'm learning Spanish now, although I didn't speak it before I went. It wasn't really necessary then as I was dealing with English parents and children, though of course it does help.

While Gillian enjoyed her six months in Spain she found it hard work and tiring and was glad to come back to England. She has also found the experience or working in the office useful, to see how the travel trade works from another angle. Office work, for her, has been a new and useful experience. Like many reps, she was initially employed from May to October, and there was no guarantee that she would be able to work in the office at the end of the season.

## Sailing Flotilla Representatives

There are many companies, both big and small, that offer more specialised holidays, such as those for the elderly, safaris in Africa, ocean-going cruises, long-haul holidays to places as far away as China and Hong Kong for example, treks in the Himalayas or the mountains of Morocco, or sailing flotillas in the Mediterranean. Along with their 'general' representatives, these companies employ representatives who may have more specialised, though not necessarily academic, qualifications.

Flotilla sailing holidays are usually offered by specialist companies, or by off-shoot branches of the big tour-operating companies. Many, though not all, of the companies offering these types of holiday do their selling directly rather than through travel agencies.

Flotillas consist of around ten yachts, which follow a route planned and led by the 'lead crew' - a flotilla leader, an engineer (sometimes both jobs are done by one person), and a 'hostess' whose job is similar to that of a resort rep, except that here the hotel is a yacht, and the clients are afloat rather than on dry land!

The hostess on a flotilla deals with airport transfers, provides a welcoming speech, and gives details of where stocks of food, and blocks of ice to put into cooler boxes for protecting food, can be purchased. She explains where the restaurants and shops are, in the same way as the resort rep does, as well as arranging social events and dealing with general queries.

## What is the Work Really Like?

The jobs that representatives do for these companies appear very attractive, taking them to 'faraway places with strange sounding names'! But the question is, are they as wonderful as they sound, or is there more to it? Andy Platt, who is 23, combines the roles of flotilla leader and engineer in the Greek Islands and off the coast of Southern Turkey.

□ The idea that this job is all just 'fun in the sun' is wrong, it's a myth - the truth is that it's very hard work, and in fact if it was just fun I would consider that I was wasting my time.

He goes on to explain that his work involves introducing himself to the clients and giving some explanations about the yachts and how to operate the engines, radios, loos and showers, as well as giving information about the sailing routes and weather. A flotilla leader, engineer and hostess often share the responsibilities of giving advice and help to clients about local facilities. Having gained experience as an engineer with the lead crew last year, Andy is using that experience as flotilla leader this year.

□ This year I am combining the engineer and skipper roles on what we call villa/flotilla holidays. This is where people spend a week ashore and then a week sailing with the flotilla. You have to be prepared to do anything that's required of you, and that means *anything*, so you must be totally flexible in this job. I am responsible for the safety of the clients and for the yachts, up to ten at a time. They are worth over £10,000 each, and the people using them sometimes appear determined to destroy themselves and the boats!

Apart from leading the flotilla there are lots of behind-the-scenes things which I help with, such as organising group activities, preparing food for barbecues, and sorting out problems for clients. These are the difficult parts of the job which no one really sees you doing. It's not easy organising 30 holiday-makers in such a way that they don't notice you doing it! You have to be sociable all the time and that can be hard, especially if you don't like a particular person, or you are just feeling 'off'. The most trying part of it is being nice all the time – having the fixed smile! You also tend to eat and drink too much; the clients are all for it so you often have to join in. It's difficult keeping a balanced diet, especially when you're away from home.

We live on board the yachts, and it tends to feel cramped after a long period of time. There aren't any set hours – you just work for as long as it takes, and if that means all night then that's how long you work! So you are really on call 24 hours a day. If any of your friends or family come out to visit, you can't expect to be with them all the time. Having said that I do get about one in three evenings off, but it's certainly not a normal life-style.

### Relationships with Other Workers

Sociability is vital in Andy's job.

☐ Usually we work in a team – skipper, engineer and hostess all working together – so you have to be able to get on if you're going to spend months together. Sometimes good relationships are established, but at other times it can be disastrous! You have to be able to get along with all kinds of people from lots of different backgrounds, and be patient with them. You can't afford to have a fast temper. You are working with people who are usually older than you, so you have to be confident and sometimes quite firm so that they respect you and your decisions. But you also need to be diplomatic: it's no good being too confident, as this can be as bad as being too shy.

## The Off-Season

Apart from being flotilla leader, Andy trained as an engineer with the Merchant Navy after he left school, and was originally employed by his company as an engineer for the yachts, which means that when the holiday season ends, his work still goes on.

☐ While it's fine in the summer months, the work in the winter is pretty grim. Even in Greece it's cold and wet, everywhere is closed and nothing is happening as the tourist season is dead. I have to get all the boats set up and prepared in the winter, and it's a dull and dirty job. This involves checking everything – the electrical and waste systems, cookers, water tanks, winches, ropes, sails, dinghies and so on – and then I have all the engines to strip and inspect.

## So What Makes it Worth Doing?

There are, however, great compensations.

☐ Admittedly in the summer it's good working in the sun. If you forget about the pressure of the work it can be very pleasant and relaxed. It's definitely good fun if you are a sociable type, and I'm working at something I enjoy – sailing. I suppose the best part of it is that it's fun when you get a good group of people together.

   However, it's not the type of job most people do for years. If you are in your fourth year you are probably becoming an old-timer! You find that the work wears you out and you can lose enthusiasm, which is very important in this job. The experience is good, though, and helps you get used to coping with people. Most of the people who do this type of work are young, because of the life-style and the amount of stamina you need. There are very few old-timers around, but those who are have usually chosen this as a way of life.

While Andy is quick to deny that it is all 'fun in the sun', he admits to one of his reasons for doing it:

☐ When I get old I want to be able to sit down by the fireside with
my grandchildren, and then I'll be able to tell them tales about
when I was sailing around the Greek and Turkish coasts
single-handed!

**Qualities Needed**
Jobs of this kind are more unusual, and Andy explains how he
came to hear about this one:

☐ These jobs – for skippers, engineers, and hostesses – are
usually advertised in the sailing magazines. Or if you are really
keen you can write direct to sailing companies and ask. You
can also make contacts at events like the Boat Shows. After
this, it's the interview that really counts in getting you the job.

Sometimes qualifications are important; they helped me to
get this job as I had qualified as a marine engineer. But for the
skipper and hostess jobs they go for personality first, and the
skipper needs to have had a lot of experience of sailing; you
need to have a strong personality to be able to cope under
pressure. For that reason they don't usually employ anyone
under 18, and they prefer you to have had experience of
working with people. It helps to be able to speak a foreign
language too, although last year we worked in Turkey and
none of us spoke Turkish. Yet you pick up quite a lot in a short
time.

## Chapter 4
# Travel Companies

Short or long journeys can involve travel by road, rail, sea or air. By sea it could be on a hovercraft or boat, by road it could be by coach, bus or car, and on the island of Santorini in Greece your taxi could be a donkey! The means of transport chosen depends on speed, convenience, distance of the journey, and cost.

In Chapter 1 it was explained how tour operators 'buy' the services of travel companies for package holidays. While some tour operators have their own airline or coach companies for example, they also use other privately or nationally owned companies for getting travellers to their destinations. Apart from the package tours, travel companies also deal with independent travellers and business people who buy their tickets as individuals.

Some companies, like the National Bus Company and British Rail, are known first as travel providers, but have developed a tour-operating side offering holidays – National Travel and Golden Rail are their tour operators and employ the same kinds of people as any other tour operator. Both privately owned and nationally owned companies may work to timetables, providing a 'scheduled' service, and they may provide a 'charter' service for groups of holiday-makers. So it sometimes happens that an air steward/ess may be working with tourists going on holiday one day and with independent and business travellers the next. Coach drivers too may be working on a scheduled route one day, and driving a group of holiday-makers on an excursion the next. .

This chapter takes a brief look at the wide variety of jobs which are available with the companies that provide travel facilities. There are other books published by Kogan Page, like *Jobs in Airports* and *Careers at Sea*, which give greater detail about the types of work available. The jobs mentioned here are those which involve most contact with the travelling public.

## Air Travel

People who work for an airline company are employed either to work on the aircraft in flight, or on the ground in an airport where they look after their company's clients. Other people work in the airport too but are employed by the operators of the airport, which may be the British Airports Authority, a local authority or the Civil Aviation Authority. Then there are airports which may be owned by a private company.

### Airports

Keeping an airport running smoothly depends on many individuals working well together to provide a range of services to passengers and to the airlines with which they are travelling. The bigger airports normally function for 24 hours a day, seven days a week and 52 weeks a year, and this involves a great number of people who have to be organised by the management. In the major airports people may be employed as one of the following: clerks, to operate switchboards, closed circuit TV and public address systems; secretaries; receptionists who provide information and assist passengers to check both themselves and their baggage in; baggage handlers who collect and take luggage to and from the planes; porters; freight handlers; caterers; nurses; car park attendants; drivers; firemen; air traffic controllers; cleaners; maintenance engineers; security staff; handling agents who ensure that the planes are fully crewed; and apron staff who work on the tarmac helping to direct the planes.

Many of these jobs do not require specific academic qualifications, although some – like air traffic control and nursing – do, and have a specific training requirement as well. Clerks and receptionists are normally expected to have some GCSEs (grades A–C) or equivalent, especially in English and maths, and for some jobs there is a minimum entry age of 18. Those who work on the information desks and on the public address systems may be expected to have A levels or the equivalent and be fluent in several languages.

Some services are 'contracted out' to specialist companies, for example to outside caterers or cleaners, which means that such staff may not be employed by the airport authority. As airports are open at all hours, many of the jobs are worked on a shift pattern, so people normally have to live close by. Anyone interested in working in an airport should write to the British Airports Authority, or to the manager of an individual airport.

## Airline Companies

There are many different airline companies operating both within the UK and from the UK to foreign destinations. They deal with package holiday-makers, independent travelling people, and business travellers. Many operate charter flights as well as the regular timetables. When an airline is asked by a tour operator to provide the 'travel' part of a holiday package, that airline is expected to look after the passengers from the time they check in at the airport until the tour operator's representative takes over at the end of the journey. While there are many different types of work done within any airline company, all companies stress that competition for jobs is 'extremely keen' and vacancies are few and far between. However, some of these jobs, with their entry requirements, are detailed below. (Actual job titles may vary from company to company.)

## CABIN CREW

Air cabin crew are the people who assist passengers by providing in-flight service, which means helping people to their seats, giving instructions about safety and what to do in case of an emergency, showing where the exit doors are and explaining the use of oxygen equipment. They also serve meals and drinks, look after passengers who become ill, deal with minor accidents, administer first aid, and sell duty-free drinks, perfume and jewellery during the flight. They may have to take special care of children, the elderly or disabled people who might be travelling alone. They are representatives of the airline and have to promote a good image of the company by being polite and helpful to their passengers and wearing the uniform which is provided for them. It is also a very demanding job, working in the narrow aisles of the aircraft, and cabin crew need to be alert and ready to act in case of emergency.

Personality is very important, therefore, and crew have to be prepared to work irregular hours, including shifts, should enjoy dealing with people, and be capable of being calm in stressful situations.

Most companies take people from 20 to about 30 years of age at the start of their training, and there is usually a height requirement – between 5ft 4in and 5ft 9in for women and 5ft 7in to 6ft 2in for men. They are also expected to have an average weight for their height. In addition, cabin crew should be able to swim and it helps to be able to speak one or more foreign languages. Although it is not essential to have high academic qualifications, most companies prefer people who have been educated up to GCSE (grade A–C) standard or equivalent. As with many jobs in the travel industry, it is personality and appearance, as well as experience of dealing with people, which count. Those who are accepted as cabin crew attend a course of training, which lasts a few weeks and covers safety and survival, gallery management, meal and bar service, first aid, make-up and deportment.

## PASSENGER SERVICES GROUND STAFF

Back on the ground, but still with the airline companies, there are staff who carry out various jobs which involve them in looking after passengers within the airport itself. This involves a whole variety of tasks such as transferring passengers from trains, coaches or other aircraft, and then through the airport controls and immigration checks. They also help passengers with enquiries about flight arrivals and departures, as well as connections with trains and coaches.

Ground staff are responsible for checking passengers in, allocating seat numbers for the flight, and looking after families with small children or babies, the elderly, the disabled and VIPs. They also check in passengers' baggage for the flight, and deal with any excess charges. Occasionally it is also necessary to look after a group of passengers waiting for a delayed flight.

Ground staff, in the same way as cabin staff, are representatives of their company and also wear a uniform. They too are normally expected to have been educated up to GCSE (grade A–C) standard, particularly in English and maths, and it helps to have had experience of working with people, such as in a shop or in catering or reception work. It is also a distinct advantage to be able to speak a European language fluently. Ground staff normally work in shifts, and some of the work is physically hard and involves a lot of walking and standing. Again, there are normally height and weight requirements for these jobs which involve a lot of contact with the public, and a minimum entry age of 20 is common, with a maximum starting age of between 30 and 35. These requirements vary slightly depending on the airline company.

## TELEPHONE SALES AGENTS

Telephone sales agents deal with reservations for seats and other enquiries over the telephone. They may deal direct with passengers or with travel agencies. While they do not deal with customers face to face they are nevertheless talking to people all the time. Their job is to provide information about fares, and methods of payment for tickets, as well as giving advice on routes, hotels, visa requirements, medical requirements, car hire and so on. Telephone sales agents are often a first point of contact for the public, and again are important in presenting an image of the company. They are also likely to work shifts. For these reasons they are usually over 18, and may be expected to be fluent in a European language, with an educational standard up to GCSE (grade A-C) or equivalent.

Enquiries about jobs with airlines should be directed to the individual companies. A comprehensive list of companies operating in the UK can be obtained from the Air Transport Industry Training Association, the address of which is given in Chapter 8.

## Bucketshops

On the subject of air travel, there are agencies commonly called 'bucketshops' which sell air tickets at prices usually well below officially agreed rates. They are able to do this because airline companies normally agree minimum prices with national governments; when they are left with unsold tickets the airline cannot break these agreements by selling off the seats more cheaply. So, while most airlines do not publicly admit to it, they allow these spare tickets to be sold at discounts through the bucketshops, rather than have empty seats on the planes. Travellers who buy tickets through a bucketshop may not have the same protection as when they go through companies registered with the Association of British Travel Agents. Nevertheless, bucketshops have been operating for years, and while most of them are found in London there are some in the provinces too, and they employ clerks and telephone sales people in a similar way to travel agencies.

## Sea Travel

Although the means of transport is different, the functions of ports and ships and hovercraft are much the same as those of airports and planes: passengers and their luggage are taken to their destinations as efficiently and comfortably as possible. People who work at ports are employed by port and harbour authorities, local authorities or privately owned companies, and the jobs they do are similar to those in airports. Shipping and hovercraft companies may also employ some staff to work at the port and others on board their vessels.

### Jobs at Sea

Cross channel ferry companies like Townsend Thoresen recruit their permanent sea staff from the Merchant Navy Establishment, which is a pool of people who have qualified as ratings or officers through Merchant Navy training. This usually means getting a shipping company's sponsorship to attend a course of training on leaving school. However, there are very few companies recruiting school-leavers at present, as the merchant fleet has been much reduced in recent years. For those who do qualify there are three main areas of work on board ship: deck work, engineering, and catering. The catering jobs are those which involve most contact with the travelling public and include cook, steward, waiter, barkeeper, shop attendant, hostess, cashier and general attendant. To join most of these jobs you should be at least 20.

Hostesses on the cross channel ferries, where there is a lot of contact with the public, need to be able to speak fluent French, although they do not necessarily need to have passed examinations in the subject. Many hostesses get experience in reception and secretarial duties in a shore-based job first. On ocean-going cruise liners there is office work which includes looking after information desks, cash handling, passenger welfare and possibly entertainments, and all this is the responsibility of pursers or assistant pursers. People who have obtained other qualifications, such as nursery nurses and hairdressers, are also employed on board the larger ships, although the waiting lists for work on board cruising ships are often up to two years long.

Many companies take on seasonal workers for the busy summer season, to work in various departments, mainly in catering or office-type work. Interviewing for these jobs usually takes place in April or May, so it can be worth enquiring about vacancies early in the year with the various cross channel shipping or hovercraft companies, as well as the many smaller ferry companies that operate round the coasts of Britain. The addresses of many of these can be found in the *ABC Shipping Guide* which is available for reference in most public libraries, or try asking a local travel agent if they have an old copy which they can spare.

SMALL SHIPS YOUTH TRAINING SCHEME
The Small Ships Training Group Association (at 11–13 Canal Road, Rochester, Kent ME2 4DS) organises a YTS for those who are keen to qualify as 'Adult Seamen'. The training includes 12 months spent at sea (spread over four to five periods), as well as time spent on shore at nautical college. After two years it is also possible for some to go on to qualify as Ships Officer. There is ten weeks' leave in the first year, and trainees who find the life-style too hard, or who suffer bad seasickness or homesickness may leave at any time.

*'Jonsue' Training Workshop.* Another YTS is available on board *Jonsue*, which is an ex-seagoing vessel in Lincolnshire. Training is given in four main areas: general maintenance/seamanship, light engineering, electrical/electronics, or catering. Placements at sea are also arranged.

Anyone wanting to apply for a YTS should make enquiries at their local careers office.

## Jobs on Shore

Apart from those employed by the port authorities, many ferry companies have their own shore staff working at a port. These include general clerks and secretaries, bookings and reservations clerks, and receptionists. Most of these jobs require applicants with a minimum of maths and English at GCSE (grade A–C) or equivalent, and those jobs which involve dealing with the public are likely to require fluency in French or another European language. Some previous experience of office work is an advantage, and many companies prefer people to be over 18 on entry.

## Coach Travel

Coach travel has become an extremely popular method of travel with tour-operating companies, but it also provides for independent travelling people who want a cheap way of getting from one place to another. Coach travel is usually much cheaper than flying and, although it obviously takes longer, it has the advantage of being able to go direct to towns, villages and hotels that planes cannot go anywhere near. Within the UK there are many privately owned coach operators who, like the National Bus Company, offer longer distance travel. Some of them also offer holiday packages or excursions and day trips, as well as being available for private hire. Even when the major part of a journey has been completed by air or by rail, it is often coaches that transfer passengers from their main journey's end to their accommodation.

All coaches need at least one driver. On long-distance journeys there may be two or three drivers who take turns, as there are regulations governing how long anyone is allowed to drive a passenger coach without taking a break. And where a group of holiday-makers is being taken to the south of France for example, there may also be a separate representative of the tour-operating company on the coach.

## Drivers in the United Kingdom

Apart from drivers on local routes, there are regular, scheduled long-distance express bus routes which criss-cross the country. A new development here is the inclusion of a hostess on some of the routes, to provide information and refreshments for passengers. Some coach operators, including the National Bus Company, have their own tour-operating company taking coach loads of holiday-makers to and from European holiday centres, or on tours. Facilities are often offered as well for hiring out coaches with a driver to take people on day trips or excursions within the UK. Additionally, some companies may organise their own excursions and then advertise them to attract individual travellers.

On excursions the driver has to look after the safety of the passengers, must keep to a specified route and time-table, make regular stops for passengers to have meals or refreshments, and may also give advice on places of interest, although a guide may be hired for this purpose. The hours the driver works may vary from day to day, but on excursions there is usually a period of rest while the passengers are off on their visit. This gives the driver a chance to put his feet up, but it may also be a little boring to wait about before completing the drive home. Hours of work are often irregular and may also involve shift work and setting off at an early hour and arriving home late.

## Long-haul Drivers

Drivers on foreign routes usually work in a team. There may be as many as three drivers where, for example, a trip involves taking a group of holiday-makers down to the South of France or to Italy. The idea is to complete the journey in the shortest possible time, while keeping within the regulations. Many of the long-distance coaches have a special sleeping compartment for the driver, built into the side of the coach with a small window, some with their own drink dispenser. There is only just enough space to stretch out and sleep, and because these compartments can only be entered from the outside of the coach, there is usually a two-way radio link with the person driving.

Drivers have a very responsible job, as they have to try and keep to their time schedule while staying within speed and safety limits. There are ferries to catch, and the drivers have to try and reach their destination neither too early nor too late, for meeting the resort representatives. They should also drive carefully to ensure the comfort of their passengers during the journey.

In order to become a coach driver, it is necessary to have a PSV (Public Service Vehicle) licence. The National Bus Company provides training courses for some drivers, while many other private coach operators expect their drivers to have obtained this licence for themselves, taking lessons and a test before applying to work for them. To qualify for a PSV licence it is normally necessary to be over 21 and to have an ordinary driving licence with a good driving record, as well as being medically fit. Drivers need to be physically fit as they have the safety of their passengers to look after, and long distance driving can be very arduous and requires a lot of concentration. Some coach drivers go into the job after having spent a period in the forces driving heavy goods vehicles.

Some coach companies have minimum and maximum height requirements for their drivers, as they have a certain size of cab to drive in. No particular academic qualifications are normally asked for, but where driving is combined with some representative work then the driver should be a cheerful, outgoing person who can cope with the occasional awkward passenger. Work on excursions or on long-distance travel usually goes to drivers with a lot of experience.

**Coach Representative/Courier**
Coach representatives or couriers are those people who accompany a group of holiday-makers to their destination, or travel around with them if they are on a touring holiday. While Stephen Riddell worked as a coach representative

for Intasun, he did not do any driving himself. The company hired its coaches from other British coach operators in the UK and, across the channel, used French companies with French drivers. Stephen describes what his work involved and the qualifications he needed for it:

□ As a representative I accompanied coaches down from their departure points in Leeds or Manchester, to the port at Dover, first of all making sure all the passengers and luggage were aboard by checking from a list that the company provided. At this point the passengers walk on to the ferry and the crew loads all the baggage, so that wasn't part of our job. On the other side of the channel we took the French coach down to Italy, the South of France, or to Spain or Austria. The main job on the other side is to organise seats as these are not allocated before setting off. I would also advise passengers on changing currency either on the ferry or at the docks, as we stopped off for meals along the French motorways and these had to be paid for individually.

Most of the actual travelling is through France and involves a tremendous number of hours of work for the reps. I used to set off at say 7.30 in the morning and get to a resort at 4 or 5 pm the following day. You would then get a couple of hours to change and eat while a local transfer coach and the resort rep took your clients off to their hotels. That coach would then bring the returning holiday-makers back and we'd set off home again. That means about 70 hours of work, and during all that time you are at the beck and call of the passengers. In the height of the season I was setting off on a Monday morning to Italy, back again Wednesday night, Thursday morning off to Spain and back on Saturday, have Sunday off and be away again on Monday! It's a very strenuous job and you get very little sleep – I got used to taking cat naps. It also interferes with your social life – you don't have much time for one! However, although the first few weeks of the season are very tiring, you do get into the routine.

You do need a good knowledge of languages, especially French. I speak French, Italian and German. I didn't need any other particular qualifications for the job, although personality is important and you do have to know how to get on with people and be able to explain things to them. When I went for my interview I was in a group of about 30 people and we had to speak, so that the interviewer could see how we got on in the group. After that there was still an individual interview to go through.

You will also need to be good at organising yourself as well as other people. While you're working you are going to a tight schedule, and you have to fit in stops for meals as well as short breaks in between. You have to be able to work without supervision and there is some paperwork to do. For example you get the schedules of passengers who are travelling with you, and these need to be checked and sent back to the office. You also have reports to write if there are any problems, like lost luggage or delays, especially if you miss the ferries. And there are reports to write about the facilities and food at the motorway stops. When there are delays it's often necessary to vary these stops and try somewhere new.

While you work on your own you do have the company of the drivers, and we usually travelled with two or three coaches more or less together, which meant we'd meet up at the service stations and have a chat with the other reps.

It is a really tiring job, but I'd lived abroad and wanted to go back to working abroad. It's the sort of job which allows you to save quite a lot of money, as you don't have time to spend anything and you often get your meals free when you bring a coach load of people into the service stations. You can also claim tax back because you are working outside the UK. Sometimes the passengers give you tips too. So it's not bad financially, but you really need to come into this kind of work because you like people - you're with them all the time.

Stephen admits that it's a very tiring job and although he enjoyed it at the time he was glad when the season came to an end. As a coach rep he used to work from May to October, and then spend the winter months working in the office assisting with the reservations work. This is a job he has now decided to do permanently as a change from being always on the move.

# Rail Travel

British Rail is one of the major travel-providing companies in the UK. While many people travel independently by rail, the Golden Rail company organises holidays and short breaks to locations, throughout Britain, sometimes combining rail and coach travel. As with any other tour-operating company Golden Rail employs booking clerks, and representatives who take care of the holiday-makers. On the continent, rail companies such as SNCF, the French Railway service, also have their own tour-operating side. The French Travel Service employs English representatives to look after passengers travelling from the channel ports to holiday spots in the south of France, the Alps or the Atlantic coast. These representatives need to speak fluent French, and have to be prepared to look after passengers, serve ready packaged meals, clean away rubbish, and allocate and make up couchettes for those sleeping overnight on the trains.

Enquiries about jobs with the railway companies should be made direct to companies such as Golden Rail or the French Travel Service. It is always worth reading the brochures that can be found in all travel agencies, from which the addresses of these companies can also be obtained.

# Car Travel

Many independent travellers, particularly business people, hire cars at the end of their main journey. There are often branches of car hire firms within airports and at the larger railway stations. Tour operators and travel agencies also arrange car hire for holiday-makers and other clients, both at home and abroad.

### Car Hire Receptionist
Claire Phillips works as a car hire receptionist at a branch of D C Cook, dealing with business travellers as well as

*Claire points out the controls of a hired car*

individuals hiring vehicles for pleasure. She had some CSEs, although these were not essential, as it is personality which really counts – her work involves dealing with people a lot of the time.

□ Most of the vehicle movement takes place between 8.30 and 10 in the morning, and 4 and 5.30 in the afternoon, so I usually arrive at my office around 8.15 to get the paperwork organised for the day. When a customer comes in I have to feel sure in my own mind that I would be happy to lend him or her may own car first! Then I get the customer to fill out the rental agreement, taking care to ensure that all the details are correct. The smallest mistake could cost the company thousands of pounds. For example, if you don't have the correct insurance details you could lose a claim if anything happens to the car. So first of all I check the customer's driving licences, then I ask whether they require our insurance cover, or whether they are using their own. Then I may need to contact their insurance company to get some details. Next we agree the cost of the rental and the amount of deposit they will leave with us. Once that is all done I take the customers round the vehicles and show them the controls and where the spare wheel is, and I also ask them to walk round the car and point out any damage (we hope there isn't any as all our cars are new!). This usually takes about 15 minutes altogether.

During all this time I usually chat with them finding out a bit about them, where they are going, and whether it's a holiday or a business trip. It's really essential to be cheerful and to show interest in what the customers are saying, so that they will hire from us next time. When customers return the cars I walk round with them again looking for any damage, but at the same time talking to them about the car's performance and asking if they have had a good trip – so that I don't make them feel like criminals! Then I check the fuel and spare wheel and return to the office with them to complete the rental agreement. This only takes about five minutes and the customers have their deposit returned.

Between 10 am and 4 pm my day is mainly taken up with paperwork and dealing with enquiries and taking reservations. There is a lot of paperwork as each rental is entered into my daily sales figures. I also have to keep a very close watch on the number of cars on hire. If I find that I have more enquiries than I can handle, I have to tell the management that I need more vehicles. Likewise, if I find I have more cars than enquiries then it is up to me to ensure that we advertise more. The work itself is very fast-moving, and if you are tired or fed up you can't crawl off into a corner and feel sorry for yourself – you always have to be cheerful and clear-headed. If you lose concentration you could easily double book a car and that would leave you with a customer in front of you and no car to give for hire!

Although it's a busy job I find my social life has improved, mainly because the company I work for runs a lot of social clubs. I enjoy it as I like meeting people from all walks of life, and you do meet a lot of people here who could be useful to know in the future. Besides this aspect, I've always had a keen interest in cars – I took a one-year course in motor mechanics at a technical college, although I didn't need that qualification for this job (but you do need to be able to drive). And there are always the funny characters too.

## Chapter 5
# Travel Agencies

Travel agencies are intermediaries, coming between and working for two sets of clients: the individuals or groups of people who buy holidays or book travel and accommodation through them; and the tour operators, and air, rail, coach and shipping companies whose holidays and tickets they sell. The main difference between working in a travel agency and for a tour or travel operator, is that the travel agency clerk deals directly with the customer, face to face over the counter, especially where the holiday trade is concerned. Business travellers do most of their booking by phone, but the personal contact is still there.

There are around 7,000 individual offices in Britain where people work in travel and tourism, about 600 of these being tour operators and the rest travel agencies. There are 2,885 travel agency companies registered with the Association of British Travel Agents (ABTA). Some of these companies are large, with many branches, and some small with perhaps just one branch. A great many of the branches are fairly small offices employing less than half a dozen people, and most are found in the high street and are rather like shops, with large display windows. However, in recent years a number have been set up within big department stores like the Co-op and W H Smiths. In a small branch office any of the staff may get involved in any of the transactions, while in a large one there may be several different departments, dealing with holiday travel, foreign exchange, and business travel.

Clerks in travel agencies combine office work with

selling. While they sell holiday packages and travel tickets, they also give a lot of advice to customers about passport, visa and medical requirements, insurance, routes and timetables, options to look at if one type of holiday is fully booked – in fact anything the customer needs to know. They spend a lot of time on the telephone making provisional bookings, and they assist their customers in filling in booking forms. (Many travel agencies also use telex machines and computers to assist with these processes.) Their work demands accuracy, and they often double check everything on the forms, such as dates, times, reference numbers and so on. They have some general office work to do as well, dealing with the post, filing letters, passing on invoices and tickets to customers, tidying up the brochure displays and putting up posters.

## Travel Agency Clerk

Caroline Macmillan is involved in all these types of work in a branch of Woodcock Travel, where she works with five other people, and is now chief clerk.

☐ In our branch there is a manager, an assistant manager, then myself and three other clerks. It's busy here and we are always on the go. I'd been interested in travel and I originally thought about being a representative, but this job came up, so I applied and got it. Our work is really all about people, that is, a great deal of our work is face to face over the counter with our clients and on the telephone. So your personality counts a lot. People may be in a hurry and difficult situations sometimes occur when you have to play it by ear. I once had a very irate lady to deal with and she nearly had me in tears! That was in the early days – you do get used to it. But you have to be able to cope with a lot of pressure, particularly if you are dealing with the business travel side. It's not that it's difficult, but business people tend to want everything doing in ten minutes; they want to go tonight, or tomorrow, and sometimes yesterday! In our branch the manager deals with a lot of the business travel. When I do it, I just take a deep breath and think to myself: 'don't panic'.

*Caroline helps a client
to complete a holiday booking form*

Apart from business travel we also deal with independent holiday-makers. People going off on holiday by themselves and making up their own itineraries can be interesting, but it doesn't actually work out cheaper for the client; you have to advise on timetables, fares, accommodation and so on.

## Computer Work
New technology plays an essential role in the travel agency.

☐ The bulk of our work involves booking package holidays, and we now do these by computer. We can also book flights that way. The tour operators are on computer as well, so we can book holidays direct. All we have to do is to switch on, and for example call up Thomson's by keying in their code. We are then connected by a separate phone line to Thomson's office. The screen then comes up with a list of quesions, to which you give an appropriate answer. When I've got a client standing beside me I can check vacancies, hotels, prices, extras and make a reservation, all within a matter of minutes. At first I was really nervous of using the computer, but it's quite straightforward.

*Computers give travel agents a direct link to make reservations with some tour-operating companies*

### Administration
There is plenty of variety in this area of office work.

☐ You find in this job that you are not doing the same thing all the time. As well as the holidays, I deal with British Rail and intercontinental rail travel, along with air tickets. Not all travel agencies do this as they need to hold a licence to issue British Rail tickets, and to be registered with the International Air Travel Association (IATA) to issue airline tickets. I enjoy dealing with the airlines and I like the independent and business travel where you have to work out the best routes and sometimes book hotels. The big hotels usually have a London agency, but for smaller ones we often use the telex system as most business hotels have telex. The only time I really use my languages, Spanish and French, is when I book hotels overseas, though it's not really essential to be able to speak foreign languages in a travel agency.

### Training and Educational Courses
There are plenty of opportunities to build up an all-round knowledge of the business.

□ I hadn't any training before coming into this work, but Woodcock's were very good with on-the-job training and sent me on a lot of courses. I did the British Airways Fare Training course, and I've done the part-time Certificate of Travel Agency Competence (COTAC). For British Airways I had to learn some basic geography, systems of coding, and how IATA divide the world into three parts; as well as knowing about the planes, lapsed flying times, minimum connecting times, how to read the manuals, issue air tickets and work out the fares. It's very interesting and you really only need to use basic arithmetic.

You are also supposed to go on one 'educational' visit a year, but it doesn't quite work out like that – I've been on two since I've been here. The tour-operating companies organise these so that you can experience what they are offering at first hand, and look at their hotels and the trips which they organise. You are generally selected to go on these on a rota basis. I'm lucky as I've been to Cuba for one visit, and to the island of Zante near Corfu. We get 'familiarised' with the place, so that we know more about it and can advise clients. We have to write a report when we come back – that's the difficult part. Although the educationals can be very hard work, I'm not complaining: I would never have gone to Cuba otherwise!

## Working Conditions and Prospects
Caroline enjoys the social life and the varied timetable.

□ Having said that, the actual job is not as glamorous as some people think. But we do have a good social life. We have a Travel Trades Club and a lot of 'do's', like promotions where the tour operators' sales representatives spend an evening telling us about the new brochures and new holidays. We learn a lot from these, and we usually have a disco afterwards. They are also useful occasions for sorting out problems, and getting to know the tour operators.

I would say that my job is very mixed. I could do anything in the course of a day, but you do find that you are always having to break off from one thing to deal with another. We follow our own clients through, but there's always work to catch up with each day. We work from 9 am to 5.30 pm, but tend to come in a bit earlier in order to keep up. We also work on Saturdays, but I enjoy having a day off during the week; it's nice to go shopping on a quiet day. I suppose it means most of your friends are at work, but I like it, and we do get some Saturdays off. We used to have a busy season, but nowadays it seems to be busy all year round more or less.

Caroline started as a junior clerk in the travel agency and has now moved up to the position of chief clerk. It is possible, therefore, to gain promotion through experience, and many branch managers have started out in the same way. Caroline's branch is average size, and the clerks there may become involved in any aspect of the work.

## Business Travel Executive

Elizabeth Lambert works for James Hill travel as a business travel executive, which is a more specialised area of work. She explains what dealing with business travel involves:

□ I work in an office above the main travel agency, with one other girl – we both do business travel. We don't usually see our clients face to face, as most of our contact with them is by telephone, so although the office atmosphere is quite quiet, it is very busy. From taking an enquiry over the phone I 'control' the booking until the clients depart for their destinations. Generally I make the reservations on the computer, quote the cost to the clients and advise of other fares available; it depends whether they wish to travel business or first class. Then, depending on the destination, I make sure they are aware of visa and health requirements and if necessary supply them with the relevant application forms. After that we may sell ancillary services, which include hotel accommodation, a car to meet them at the airport, and continental rail tickets if travel over land is involved. Most of our work is by telephone, although we can reserve air travel through the computer, and we use telex to make hotel reservations and to confirm an itinerary to the client.

Business travel is a very competitive market and we often receive calls from companies for a quote. You know that they are ringing all the agencies in the area and that the cheapest fare will get the business. So it's up to us to be on the ball regarding all the latest special offers. For example, using a certain airline will allow the customer special rates on hotel accommodation or free car hire for a week at the destination.

## Qualities needed

Enthusiasm is vital.

☐ Although our work is mostly on the phone, personality is important too. Apart from a good telephone manner, you should appear friendly, and patience is a virtue as trips may be altered several times over. I don't speak any foreign languages, but European languages are helpful as it is not unusual to have to ring the continent to make hotel reservations. On the whole I enjoy the challenges of this job; each phone call brings a different enquiry, whether it is for a rail ticket or a quote for a round-the-world ticket! It is sometimes difficult though to keep up with all the changes that take place on a daily basis, like airlines reducing fares and all the special offers. And even though most of our work is over the phone, we find we normally have a good relationship with our clients. If anything goes wrong or the clients have a problem while they are away, we are often the first person they contact. For example, we have had several clients who have had their credit cards and money stolen. One gentleman went swimming and came out of the water to find that all his belongings had been stolen! So he contacted us and we arranged credit at the hotel and cash to be collected from an airline office. Fortunately he did have a change of clothing!

## Making a Start

Elizabeth explains how she established herself in the industry:

☐ I had some experience of dealing with business travel with another company before coming here and I had also spent two years doing a business studies course with travel and tourism options. Then I spent six months in the holiday part of the travel business before moving on to the business side. Business travel is not something that you normally do straight away; you need some experience first.

Most travel agency clerks start on booking package holidays and progress on to the more complex work of making travel arrangements for business people. Travel agencies employ young people from the age of 16 upwards and most now take school-leavers on to a Youth Training Scheme. Most agencies encourage their trainees or employees to take further qualifications by attending a college of further education or technical college. Details of schemes and courses are given in Chapter 8.

*Chapter 6*
# Tourism in Britain

Tourism is big business in the UK, partly because of the large numbers of foreign visitors to this country, but also because of the number of local people who take holidays, short breaks, excursions and day trips throughout the year, to places of interest in Britain. Tourism here includes educational tours, business trips, in fact anything that involves people going away from home for any length of time. In 1969 the government passed the Development of Tourism Act, which led to the setting up of three national tourist boards, for England, Scotland and Wales, and in addition the British Tourist Authority (BTA) to develop tourism in the UK. The BTA has a special responsibility to promote Britain to visitors coming from overseas, and now works very closely with the English Tourist Board.

The three national tourist boards have in turn a responsibility for regional tourist boards, of which there are twelve in England, three in Wales, and nine in Scotland. Although these boards do not employ large numbers of people, they collect vast amounts of information and do a great deal of research work, publicity, and brochure and guide writing – in an effort to encourage visitors to their areas. This information goes out to individuals, who make direct enquiries by telephone or by post, but also to the many Tourist Information Centres throughout the UK, so that callers to these centres have quick and easy access to it. The Information Centres are run either by local authorities or by the regional boards, and they employ information assistants or receptionists, who are the people meeting the visiting public face to face.

## Information Receptionists in London

Before taking a general look at the work of an information assistant in a Tourist Information Centre, it is worth seeing how the London Visitor and Convention Bureau (LVCB) organises its information centres. London, being the capital of Great Britain, is a special case and the LVCB has been set up to promote London to overseas as well as local people, and to encourage organisations to use the capital as a base for national and international conferences and exhibitions.

Information receptionists are employed on a full- or part-time basis in the centres situated throughout London. Their work involves dealing with enquiries from personal callers, or by post or phone from anywhere in the UK or abroad. They also provide an accommodation-finding service, making reservations for hotel or other accommodation in the London area. They hold stocks of guide books, maps and other pamphlets and books which they sell to the public, and also make bookings for sightseeing trips, visits to exhibitions and so on. As the work involves selling, they have to deal with the cash takings.

The receptionists in London usually work shifts, although a few work regular weekly hours. They have to be able to speak two European languages at a conversational level, in addition to English, and have a good standard of education, although there are no fixed academic requirements. Applicants for jobs are expected to have a thorough knowledge of London and the rest of the British Isles and to have an aptitude for figure work. Receptionists can be either male or female and should be between 18 and 45. It also helps to have had some background in sales work. While vacancies for permanent jobs are few and far between, most people start off by taking seasonal work during the busy summer months when extra staff are taken on.

## Tourist Information Assistants

Outside the London area there are hundreds of other tourist information centres, employing information receptionists or assistants. The entry requirements and the types of work done vary from place to place. Sonia Brooke, for example, works as an information assistant in a tourist information office in the small town of Holmfirth in Yorkshire – 'Last of the Summer Wine' country! Sonia has found that the television programme filmed in the locality has increased the number of visitors to the area, and it becomes especially busy in the summer, with coach loads of visitors descending on the town. She explains how this affects her work:

☐ We're fairly quiet in the winter, but during the school holidays we get families coming in. And in term times too we get school parties. Then in the busy season we get loads of different people, including Americans, Australians, French, Japanese, Germans – anyone. Some people are here to see relatives, while others are just visiting.

The office Sonia works in is rather like a shop or a travel agency, with an attractive window display of books, leaflets and posters, all advertising local as well as national events and places of interest. She explains that most of her work is based in the office itself, but that this is very varied:

☐ There are no two days the same. When it's quiet in the winter I spend a lot of time setting up the displays, sorting out the books and leaflets. The leaflets are mainly free, but the books are for sale. Having to keep the shelves stocked is a routine chore, but it's also a way of getting to know the literature. In the winter I do a lot of checking to make sure it's all up to date. I also make out lists, for all sorts of things – for hotels or local mills. I'm not allowed to give advice on the standards of accommodation, but I can tell people where the hotels and guest-houses are. You only have to be asked a few times for such information and you find it's easier to have it on a list to give out. You need to listen to the questions you are asked – I've got a fair idea of the sorts of things people want to know, so I can use my wit to make life easier.

I write off for the information both from round here and from further afield, as local people come in for information too. I get leaflets about fun fairs, historic buildings – anything. There is a lot of information to deal with; in this job you have to be ready to answer absolutely any question. I don't always know the answers, but I usually know where or how to find out. You are expected to know about everything from heart surgery to how to get to Hong Kong! I have a stock of books and guides here, many of which are produced by the English Tourist Board, and the Yorkshire and Humberside Tourist Board. They send out leaflets and other information sheets to us regularly.

A lot of my time is spent on clerical work, as I do the filing of spare copies of literature, and I have to keep stock and sales returns for the books and maps. I also type all my own letters. I have to be a jack of all trades as I'm the only full-time tourist assistant in this office! However, I do work with other people as I'm employed by the local council and my particular office is a combined one. People come in to pay their rates here, so I help with some cashier work during the quiet winter months.

In summer I spend most of my time dealing with customers. Sometimes whole coach loads come in at a time, and then I tend to get up and address the whole crowd, to save repeating the same thing over again. They ask all kinds of questions, like Where is Nora Batty's house or Sid's Café? so it helps if I've been to see some of these places myself, and I do occasionally go out to have a look at something.

## Qualities Needed

Most people who come into this type of work are expected to have some GCSEs at grade A–C or equivalent. It is not uncommon to be asked for around four GCSE passes, although it is not always necessary to be able to speak a foreign language. While many of Sonia's visitors are from overseas, she explains that she does not often need to be able to speak a foreign language – though she can 'get by' in French:

❑ I reckon that most visitors who can find us this far up in Yorkshire can usually manage the language! It's more important to like people in this job. I'm meeting new people all the time and I enjoy helping them. They're usually nice, although there's the occasional one you'd like to strangle! Mostly, it's a case of listening to them and responding to what they want, and then there are the locals who also come in for a chat. Whoever it is, your customers always have to come first; whatever I'm doing when someone comes in, I drop it to deal with them. I don't think it's the sort of job you can do well straight from school. You really need to be experienced with people first, to have dealt with cash, and to know some geography – it helps if you know where Scotland is!

## Training

As part of your in-service training, it is possible to go on courses leading to qualifications.

☐ There isn't any particular training for my work. I was trained on the job. But there is a qualification that information assistants can work towards, which is the Certificate of Tourist Information Centre Competence (COTICC), and I shall be doing this by going to college two days a week for about a month. The qualification will help me if I want to apply for promotion or for other jobs in tourism later on. The only other training I have had is a two-day 'familiarisation' trip which was arranged by the Yorkshire and Humberside Tourist Board. The idea is that they take you somewhere to look at the local places of interest and to stay in a hotel, so that you can see at first hand what it is all about.

As tourism develops in Britain, training for work in the industry becomes more important, and a greater range of courses is becoming available for those who work in tourist information offices, stately homes, or with guide or tour companies for example. Many of these courses are taken on a part-time basis, or while working, as 'in-service' courses.

Many jobs in tourist information are taken up by people who have had some other type of work experience before applying, but it can also help to have been on a Youth Training Scheme, or on a college course with travel and tourism options.

## Tourist Guides

Tourist guides are important people in the development of tourism at home. It is they who take visitors round to see the sights, and introduce them to places of interest on an organised basis. In order to do a good job, they need detailed knowledge of an area and its attractions. They may be employed by guide companies, or by one of the local authorities or tourist boards. Alternatively, they may work on a freelance basis, being paid for the jobs they do rather than working full time for one organisation.

Ann Dixon works as a tourist guide in what at first sight appears an unlikely tourist area – the industrial city of Bradford in Yorkshire. However, Bradford Metropolitan Council take their tourist trade seriously and have employed a tourism and conferences officer to promote holidays, visits and conference facilities in the area, which attracts large numbers of people: those who are interested in the city's historical development at the heart of the textile industry, and those who come to visit the surrounding dales and moorland. When the number of visitors began to increase, a decision was taken to train a number of guides. An article in the local paper attracted over 400 replies, from which 40 people were taken on to a ten-week course. Training was given on a part-time basis, on one evening a week and on Saturdays. Ann was one of those who responded to the newspaper article, and she has now been working for four years as a freelance guide through the main tourist season, from April to October. She was not asked for any particular academic qualifications, but did need to be enthusiastic about the area:

□ I used to work as a designer of garments in the woollen hosiery trade, so I had a knowledge of the clothing trade, and I'm locally born and bred, so I know the area well. I took the ten-week course which was arranged by the Council, and I've also done a three-day course on York Minster, a three-month course on Leeds, and a six-month course on Yorkshire. You have to take exams at the end of all these courses. It's hard

*A 'Blue Badge' guide*
*welcomes holiday-makers to Bradford*

work, but worth it as I now have my 'Blue Badge' and am registered as a guide with the Yorkshire and Humberside Tourist Board.

I organise a lot of day excursions. These might be for clubs, or for coach or tour companies. I get paid for them on a daily fee. The client usually arranges where we are going and I accompany the visitors. For example, I might join the coach in Bradford, to take a group round the mill shops, up to 'Bronte' country to see the museums and other sights. Before I set out, I usually type an itinerary for them, book lunch, and cost up the excursion. So there's quite a lot of organisation and paperwork involved before a trip takes place. I'm not keen on the office side of the work, and it can be difficult to chase after work as that really involves asserting yourself. However, most of the work is done on the coaches, although sometimes I guide a walking tour. I work on my own, so I don't usually see other guides. The people I have contact with are the customers, so it's here today and gone tomorrow! But it is nice to meet all the different people.

## Working Conditions

Few guides are able to work on a full-time permanent basis. Those who have the blue badge qualification are listed in publications giving details of local guides. Tour operators or other people organising excursions then contact a guide direct when they require their services. Ann goes on:

☐ It's very seasonal and very part time, and I have to work unsociable hours, like at the weekends, but this is okay for me as my children have now grown up. Sometimes I work for seven days one week and then find I'm doing nothing for the next three weeks. But I do enjoy the variety, and I like not being tied to regular hours. I get about the countryside and I'm working in the fresh air. It's also nice to be able to organise your own work and to decide for yourself what limits you work within. Most of all I like helping people to enjoy themselves and being able to show them interesting places. One middle-aged lady who came with us on the coach excursion to Haworth, home of the Brontes, told me that it had been the best day of her life!

## Training

The training that guides receive varies from area to area. Courses, some of which last for a few months, are usually run on a part-time basis by tourist boards, colleges, local councils and other organisations, and lead to the award of the Blue Badge. The Guild of Guide Lecturers and the British Incoming Tour Operators' Association advise on the selection, training and examination of guides, and the Guild keeps a list of registered guides which it circulates to tour operators, tourist information centres and other potential employers.

The training itself can be quite rigorous. In London, for example, guides study history, geography, architecture, art, music, theatre, literature, and also receive practical help with voice production, microphone techniques, practical guiding and first aid. In some cases, particularly in the London area, it is necessary for guides to be fluent in a

◀ *Promotional work in the Bronte town of Haworth*

foreign language too. While formal qualifications are not always asked for, the training does involve a lot of study, and the work itself requires guides who are mature and reliable, have a lot of patience and stamina, and enjoy working with groups of people.

# Part 2

## Chapter 7
# Entry and Training

There are three main ways of getting into travel and tourism on leaving school:

- [] getting permanent employment, where experience can be supplemented by day-release courses of study;
- [] spending a year or two on a Youth Training Scheme (YTS);
- [] going to a college of further education, or a technical college, for a year or two and obtaining qualifications in travel and tourism.

These are direct options to consider. However, as has been shown earlier in this book, there are many jobs which require people to be more mature and which are not therefore normally open to school-leavers. So there is a fourth option:

- [] gain some experience of working with people in another kind of job, and then apply for a post such as overseas representative.

Each of these options is considered in this chapter. But it should be remembered that there is no one correct route into the business and every choice will depend on an individual's circumstances and also on what is offered locally. Careers officers and careers teachers can offer advice on this choice to young people leaving school, as well as to adults who are considering a career change.

## Employment

Most people who go into the travel business straight from

school, go into clerical jobs. While there are no rigid academic entry requirements, most firms ask for up to four or five GCSE grades A–C or equivalent. The most useful subjects to have studied are English, maths, a foreign language and geography, although other subjects are also taken into account. Of course it is also possible to obtain clerical jobs after having spent a year or two at a college obtaining further qualifications, like those mentioned in the section on courses later in this chapter.

Clerical jobs are available with tour operators, travel agencies, regional or national tourist boards, tourist information centres, ferry, airline or coach companies, and car hire firms. There is always a lot of competition for permanent jobs, and some employers prefer to take young people who have spent time on a Youth Training Scheme or who have taken a course of full-time study first, although there are no rules about this.

For other work, which is not clerical, such as the representative jobs, most employers prefer to take people who are more mature and who have already had some experience of dealing with people, so it can be useful to have worked in a shop, as a nurse, or in any other job where there is a lot of contact with the public.

## Entry Requirements

The jobs listed below are just a few examples of the type of work available in travel and tourism, which have been looked at in this book. Brief notes are given here of the academic entry requirements, normal minimum age on entry, the type of personality that employers tend to look for and any language requirements. Different companies may have different requirements, and many people start off in some of these types of work by taking a seasonal job, so these notes are intended as a guide only and full details should be obtained from individual companies. Although the entry requirements here are expressed as GCSEs at grades A–C, other equivalent qualifications, such as the

Scottish certificates or BTEC and SCOTVEC qualifications, are also acceptable.

Nearly all positions in travel and tourism require an ability to get on with people, and this applies to both the administration and representative sides. Aside from this common factor, the entry requirements for each job are denoted in the following way: the first figure stands for the number of GCSE (grade A–C) needed (where there are no minimum academic qualifications specified this is stated as a – ); the second figure denotes the minimum entry age; last, where a foreign language would be an advantage this is expressed FL, and where it is essential **FL**.

*Reservations/bookings clerk:* 2–5 (although some companies ask for higher qualifications); 18.

*General clerk in smaller tour-operating company:* 2–5; 16 (some companies prefer 18).

*Overseas/resort representative:* –; 20–22; **FL**.

*Children's representative:* no minimum academic qualifications are specified but many candidates are expected to have the National Nursery Examination Board certificate. The NNEB may be taken at 18, although 'kiddie' reps may be expected to be older. Obviously you must also like children.

Other representatives, such as flotilla leaders, trek leaders and ski guides, require no particular academic qualifications but should obviously offer the relevant specialist skills. Recruits are not normally taken on below 18, and some companies prefer them to be over 20. A foreign language is not always essential.

*Air cabin crew:* GCSE (grades A–C) preferred; 20; FL.

*Passenger services ground staff:* GCSE (grades A–C) preferred; 18–20; FL.

*Telephone sales agent:* GCSE (grades A–C) preferred; 18; FL.

*Clerk/administrative assistant:* GCSE (grades A–C) preferred; 16.

*Coach driver:* should be over 21 and have a Public Service Vehicle licence (PSV).
*Coach rep/courier:* –; 20; **FL**.
*Information assistant (tourist information centre):* 2-5; 18; **FL** in London, FL elsewhere.
*Guide:* –; 20; FL; should be acquainted with area to be covered.
*Travel agency clerk:* 2-5; 16; FL.

## In-service Training

Once in employment, there are day-release and evening courses available, which lead to qualifications in business studies with travel and tourism options. These may take the form of the Business and Technician Education Council's general and national certificates (BTEC), or the Scottish equivalent offered by the Scottish Vocational Education Council (SCOTVEC), or the Certificate of Travel Agency Competence (COTAC). In addition, there is the Certificate of Tour Operating Practice (COTOP), the Certificate of Tourist Information Centre Competence (COTICC), and the Visitor Attraction Practice Certificate, all of which are certificated by the City and Guilds of London Institute. The Open College is also expected to be offering a course entitled 'An Introduction to Tourism in Britain' to those who are already in employment or who will be seeking employment in travel and tourism. These qualifications are explained, with their entry requirements, later in this chapter in the section on courses of study.

Training does not stop once you are in employment, as there are large numbers of courses available to people in the business. These are offered by companies such as British Airways, Sealink and others, and cover all aspects of air or sea ticketing. The companies award their own certificates to those who pass. City and Guilds also offer the Travel Licensing Certificates which cover rail travel in the UK and Europe and air travel. These certificates are recognised by British Rail and by the International Air

Transport Association (IATA). For those involved in tourist information work, there is the Certificate of Tourist Information Centre Competence (COTICC) course (examined by the City and Guilds of London Institute), which can be taken as a short course while in employment. The syllabus covers the nature and structure of tourism and its organisation in the UK, information acquisition, storage and retrieval, local knowledge and places of interest, cash handling, customer contact, and the display and promotion of material.

A newer qualification can now be taken by those who work in tourist attractions such as stately homes and theme parks. This is the Visitor Attraction Practice Certificate (CGLI 489).

### Finding Companies

Anyone wanting to go straight into a permanent job should write and make enquiries about the possibility of employment to individual travel agencies, tour operators, ferry companies, coach companies, airlines, or tourist boards. Some useful addresses can be found in Chapter 8. The addresses of the main tour-operating companies are contained in their brochures, which are available in the travel agencies. It is also worth looking through the brochures to see what kinds of holidays and services these tour operators offer.

More and more employers are taking people on as YTS trainees first rather than offering permanent employment immediately. Therefore, it is well worth while for school- and college-leavers to consider this option.

### Youth Training Schemes

Youth Training Schemes usually last for two years, paying an allowance of £28.50 per week in the first year, and £35.00 per week in the second year, and are available with travel agencies, tour operators and others involved in the travel business throughout Great Britain. Other schemes are 'college-based', which means that a college offers training, involving some periods of practical experience with employers in different sections of the industry.

There are no minimum qualifications for getting on to schemes, although it does help to have studied English, maths, a language and geography at school. During the time spent on a YTS, experience can be gained in different departments of a company and it is normal to study by part-time day release for business studies qualifications or for the travel and tourism certificates mentioned earlier in this chapter.

### Tour Operators

Tour-operating companies like Intasun and Thomson take YTS trainees, who may work in such areas as reservations and bookings, bookkeeping and accounting, and keyboard and computer skills. This is one way of gaining experience in departments which do not normally take people on until they are 18. Individual companies organise their own training programmes, so it is necessary to contact these companies directly to make enquiries about whether they operate a YTS.

Incoming tour operators who deal with visitors coming to Britain, rather than British visitors, also take YTS trainees on placements in their offices. The training covers a range of general office work, including computer skills and simple accounting. The training also looks at the background to tourism (to see why visitors are attracted to the UK), the backgrounds of the different visiting tourists, as well as teaching trainees how to use reference materials and how to deal with clients and cope with travel terminology. The training will be relevant to those who want to work with incoming tour operators, or with coach companies, hoteliers, regional tourist boards, or in airports, port authorities and ferry companies.

### Travel Agencies

Travel agencies take YTS trainees to gain experience in the

work of a counter clerk. Again, they learn general office skills, including dealing with customers over the counter, and using computerised systems that are linked to individual tour-operating companies for making bookings. They also learn how to deal with reservations clerks by telephone.

The main YTS for travel agency work is organised and managed by the Association of British Travel Agents on behalf of individual travel agency companies. Applications should, therefore, go direct to ABTA who organise local placements for trainees accepted for the scheme. ABTA explain that getting on to a Youth Training Scheme with them is as competitive as getting a job, because 94 per cent of ABTA YTS trainees end up with permanent full-time employment within the industry. Not every travel agency is involved in the scheme yet, so it is still worth while contacting local ABTA travel agents and asking if they will act as a sponsor for it. Other organisations also have YTS placements in travel agencies, so it is always worth checking with careers offices to find out where these are.

Apart from those schemes where the trainee is based in a travel agency and attends college for further study, there are the schemes which are college-based but with periods spent out in the industry to gain practical experience. Schemes which are approved by ABTA are run at the colleges listed in Chapter 8 (this list was correct at the time of printing, but may have expanded – an up-to-date list can be obtained from ABTA).

## Courses of Study

Colleges of further education and technical colleges throughout the UK offer a wide range of courses which have been approved by ABTA or the Institute of Travel and Tourism (ITT) as offering a full range of travel and tourism options. If there is any doubt whether a course has this approval, ABTA and ITT will answer enquiries. (Their addresses are provided in Chapter 8.)

Courses which can be entered with up to four GCSEs (grades A–C) or equivalent are courses of further education, which means that full maintenance grants are not normally available from local authorities, although tuition fees are usually paid. Most school-leavers therefore must consider courses at colleges local to them. Some of the qualifications which are useful in the travel industry are described here, with their entry requirements. Most of the qualifications described in this section can be taken as full-time or as part-time courses of study. The part-time courses are mainly designed for those people who are already in employment or on a YTS.

Chapter 8 contains a list of colleges which offer one or other of these qualifications. Full details of the course content can be obtained direct from individual colleges. Applications should be made as early as the autumn term in the year before entry.

**Certificate of Travel Agency Competence (COTAC)**
The syllabus for this certificate is set by ABTA and covers air fares and ticketing as one part of the course. It also looks at general travel, and this includes package holidays, coach and rail transportation, hotels, car hire, finance, insurance, traveller's cheques and currency, passports, visas and health requirements. It is examined by the City and Guilds of London Institute (CGLI). While it is normally offered as a part-time course to those who are in employment or on a YTS, there are also a few colleges which offer it as a full-time course which can be taken along with the BTEC/SCOTVEC national diploma or the Certificate in Travel Studies in some colleges. The certificate has two parts, the first of which is taken after a year of study. There are no specific entry requirements for the course, and those colleges offering the certificate are listed in Chapter 8.

### Certificate of Travel Agency Competence (CGLI 495) (COTAC)

This certificate is offered at two levels which can be taken one after the other. It can be taken while on a YTS or while taking a full-time college course, along with a BTEC course for example. It can also be taken by using self-study materials provided by ABTA for those who are in employment. Those who pass the COTAC level 1 course can use the letters CertTS after their names as they are eligible for the Certificate in Travel Agency Skills. After getting COTAC level 2 they can use the letters DipTS. Level 1 aims at providing the basic competence required by a counter clerk in a travel agency; and level 2 aims to widen knowledge and ability.

The course is designed for people who are new to the industry and covers air fares and ticketing, finance, insurance, travellers' cheques, currency, passports and visa and health regulations.

### Certificate in Travel Studies (CGLI 499)

The Certificate in Travel Studies is a fairly new one-year full-time course, which requires no formal entry qualifications, but entrants are expected to be literate, numerate, and have a good knowledge of geography. The certificate is equivalent in level to COTAC level 1. It covers background to the industry, tour operations, travel geography, structure of tourism, and marketing and selling skills. In addition, the COTAC level 1 syllabus is covered. Other practical skills are included, such as information technology, office skills and personal attributes.

### Certificate of Tour Operating Practice (COTOP) (CGLI 497)

This is a relatively new qualification, which is offered at two levels, and it can be taken part time or full time at a small number of colleges. Level 1 gives an understanding of the function of a tour operator, covering structure and organisation of the UK travel industry, an outline of the development of the inclusive tour, the role of the brochure and topics concerned with the business environment of the tour operator. Level 2 goes further with a detailed knowledge and understanding of the business practices appropriate to tour operating, including the planning, production, pricing and marketing of the inclusive tour.

## Certificate of Tourist Information Centre Competence (COTICC) (CGLI 492)

This is a part-time qualification which is usually taken by those who work in tourist information centres. It includes storage and retrieval of information, operating sales outlets, organisation and structure of the tourism industry, local and non-local knowledge, display and promotion skills, and the interpersonal skills of customer contact.

## Visitor Attraction Practice (CGLI 489)

This is a qualification which is aimed at those who work in places like stately homes or theme parks. The scheme covers all the main topics of day-to-day operation, including sales interpretation and presentation of skills, as well as an introduction to tourism. This is a new qualification and is currently offered at only a small number of colleges.

## Open College Tourism Courses

### AN INTRODUCTION TO TOURISM IN BRITAIN (CGLI 480)

This new course is being planned for those who already work in the industry, as well as for those who intend to work in it. The course will be offered as part of the Open College programme through a series of television programmes, which will be accompanied by learning materials amounting to ten modules. All students will have access to a tutor, either through their workplace or through an accredited centre – by telephone if not direct. Students will have the option of obtaining the qualification above, and then going on to take the Certificate in Visitor Attraction Operations.

## Business and Technician Education Council and Scottish Vocational Education Council Diplomas/Certificates (BTEC and SCOTVEC)

These Councils validate and examine business studies courses, some of which include options on travel and tourism. Most of these courses are at the national level, which usually requires four GCSEs (grades A–C) or the equivalent for entry.

Full-time BTEC courses normally have 12 modules, of which six are compulsory 'core' subjects. Courses which include at least five of the travel and tourism modules are 'approved' by ABTA. The six travel and tourism options are: travel and tourism 1 and 2; travel geography; retail travel operations; tour operations; and sales and marketing for travel and tourism. SCOTVEC courses include the following modules: travel agency practice 1, 2 and 3; travel and tourism geography 1 and 2; travel and tourism; communication 4; office organisation and information processing; statistics; and an introduction to economic analysis, in addition to other business studies options. It is advisable to check whether a course has been approved by ABTA or the Institute of Travel and Tourism (ITT). A full list of colleges that run approved courses can be obtained from ABTA, and other details about BTEC, SCOTVEC and City and Guilds can be gained by writing to them direct (addresses on page 95). There is also a list of relevant colleges in Chapter 8.

## Gaining Experience

Many jobs in travel and tourism require people who are older, with a more mature attitude and some experience of working with people. So if it is not possible to get into the business immediately on leaving school or college, what other options are there for the 16- to 17-year-old, and how can relevant experience be gained?

## Other Relevant Qualifications

Other qualifications can prove useful – such as the National Nursery Examination Board (NNEB), which Gillian, the children's representative, took; or Merchant Navy engineering qualifications which Andy, the flotilla engineer, took. But courses in hotel and catering, or in general business studies, reception or nursing, can also be turned to good use in travel and tourism. Qualifications do not necessarily need to be academic – those who have a particular expertise, such as in climbing, hill walking, skiing or other outdoor pursuits, may also find that this experience can be used in a number of jobs.

## Getting Experience

Experience of working with people is also often expected by employers in the industry. This can be gained after leaving school or college and before reaching the minimum age for some of the jobs, like overseas representative or steward/stewardess. Many people pick up this kind of experience through working in shops, hotels, restaurants, or any job involving contact with the public.

## Seasonal Work at Home or Abroad

While competition for permanent jobs in travel and tourism is always keen, there are often seasonal jobs for people who can take short-term work. Any experience gained in this way will be useful, such as helping at a holiday camp or a hotel. It may also be worth considering voluntary work to gain experience, during school or college holidays or while looking for a permanent position. Many seasonal jobs can be found in the tourist areas of Great Britain, so it may be necessary to go to these tourist spots for summer work or, for example, to the Scottish Highlands for the winter sports season.

Vacancies are normally advertised in local newspapers or, alternatively, those who are interested can write direct to hotels and holiday camps. The addresses of many of these bodies can be found in the tourist information booklets published by the national and regional tourist boards. There are also other very useful books giving details of seasonal and holiday jobs in Britain and abroad, and some of these are listed in Chapter 8.

## Salaries and Other Benefits

People working in a *tour operator's* office (bookings/ reservations clerks) or in *travel agencies* (counter clerks) – outside London – may expect to receive around £80 per week at 18. Salaries depend on age and experience and are likely to be similar to those which other office workers, such as bank or building society clerks, receive. Most travel agency clerks and reservations/bookings clerks are offered holidays at reduced rates through their own company. Some also work 'bonus schemes', where clerks are paid extra according to how many holidays are sold.

*Tourist information assistants* are usually paid on the clerical scales which apply to the local authority or tourist board by whom they are employed. Weekly pay is around £80 at 18, but is higher in the London area.

*Overseas representatives.* Again, salaries vary, both with the job and with the employer. Some overseas representatives are 'self-employed' but work for one company for a set period, usually for one season at a time. Others are employed by a company, but again this may be for one season at a time. Some are able to get permanent contracts which allow them to work throughout the year, although they may work as reps during the summer and go into the office during the winter. Pay ranges from £70 to £150 per week, and this is usually paid into the rep's bank account at home in the UK. Some employees, such as coach reps, may be paid for each trip they do, and are often also given an extra allowance to cover meals and other expenses. There are some 'perks', such as travel allowances and concessions on holidays. Many overseas reps also get commission on the number of excursions they sell to clients.

*Guides*. Very few guides are employed full time. Many are called out to work on a particular trip, or excursion. They are normally paid a rate for the day, which varies according to the area of the country and the particular employer. They often work on a 'freelance' basis, which means that they do not have one employer, but may work for several different organisations.

## Progress within the Industry

The industry is a developing one, in which most of the people who have progressed to higher administrative and management positions have done so through their ability and their experience, rather than by having high-grade paper qualifications. While there are many in-service short courses which it helps to have taken, it is still an industry where experience in clerical/bookings/reservations, overseas or sales representative work can be used as a step up to higher levels.

As far as travel agencies are concerned there are very many small branches, each with its own manager, so many people do work up from being a travel agency clerk, to becoming manager of a branch. In tour operating, it is also possible to use experience gained in clerical or representative work to move upwards into research, development and planning. And those who gain experience in brochure writing may later find it possible to move into other areas of writing – there are many new travel publications appearing on newsagents' shelves, where experience of the travel trade and an ability to write can be used.

## Making Applications

### College Courses
When applying for college courses, it is useful to obtain prospectuses from local colleges and to read them thoroughly. Some of the colleges listed in Chapter 8 offer more

than one type and level of course with travel and tourism options, so you should check their entry requirements. If a course with travel and tourism options is not offered by a college within one local authority, it may be possible to attend a college in a neighbouring authority. Applications should be made early, preferably by around Christmas in the year before the course starts. Most colleges invite applicants for an interview during the spring term, so most people know by Easter or thereabouts whether they have been accepted for a course. It is always a good idea to discuss these applications with a careers officer, who may suggest applying for both a college course and a YTS scheme in order to keep options open.

## YTS Schemes

Local careers offices have details of the schemes available and careers officers will give advice to school- and college-leavers on how to apply. For travel agency schemes, the application should be made centrally to ABTA who arrange local placements. Also check with the careers office to find out about other organisations with place-ments for YTS in travel agencies. For college-based YTS schemes application should be made direct to the college. Many tour operators organise their own YTS, so applica-tions for these should be sent to individual tour operators. As the situation with the YTS is constantly changing it is wise to keep in close contact with a careers officer, who will have up-to-date information.

## Job Applications

Permanent jobs are advertised in local newspapers and the various travel magazines, some of which are produced for the trade. The more specialised jobs are also advertised in the special interest magazines, like the skiing, sailing and trekking magazines, which are on sale in most newsagents' shops.

Your letter of application may be in response to an advertisement, or perhaps a purely speculative one off your own bat. Whatever the form, it should contain a brief covering note, explaining your interest in both travel and tourism in general as well as the particular company, and a curriculum vitae which provides details of your career to date. The cv may take the following form:

| |
|---|
| Name                    Address<br>Telephone number |
| Schools attended<br><br>Examination passes<br><br>Training courses or colleges attended,<br>with any certificates gained<br><br>Job experience, including part-time work |
| Interests and hobbies<br><br>Positions of responsibility and honours won<br><br>Driving licence (if you have one) |
| Names and addresses of two people who can<br>give you a reference |

Getting into the travel industry is not easy; it often has a glamorous image and there is a lot of competition for jobs. But this is also true of many other industries, so is not a reason by itself for giving up. If in doubt, career plans should be discussed with parents, careers teachers in schools, and with a careers officer. Their advice can help, and if one course of action does not succeed they will be able to suggest alternatives, until a way in is found.

# Courses and Useful Addresses

The lists of colleges which appear on the following pages are those which offer courses that have been fully approved by ABTA. The qualifications obtained from these colleges will lead towards membership of the Institute of Travel and Tourism. Other colleges also offer courses with travel and tourism options, but if these have not obtained ABTA aproval, it may not be possible to obtain membership of the ITT. Courses which have not been approved by ABTA may only offer one or two of the travel and tourism options, so care should be taken when choosing a college course. A full and up-to-date list of the college courses approved by ABTA may be obtained by writing to ABTA at the address given on page 93.

## College-based YTS Schemes

**Amersham**
Amersham College of Further Education, Art and Design, Stanley Hill, Amersham, Buckinghamshire HP7 9HN

**Belfast**
Rupert Stanley College, Tower Street, Belfast BT5 4FH

**Belvedere**
Erith College of Technology, Tower Road, Belvedere, Kent DA17 6JA

**Birmingham**
Birmingham College of Food and Domestic Arts, Summer Row, Birmingham B31 1JB

**Bolton**
Bolton Metropolitan College, Manchester Road, Bolton, Lancashire BL2 1ER

**Bristol**
Soundwell Technical College, St Stephens Road, Soundwell, Bristol BS16 4RL

**Cardiff**
South Glamorgan Institute of Higher Education, Colchester Avenue, Cardiff CF3 7XR

**Carshalton**
Carshalton College of Further Education, Nightingale Road, Carshalton, Surrey SM5 2EJ

**Coventry**
Henley College of Further Education, Henley Road, Bell Green, Coventry, West Midlands CV2 1ED

**Crewe**
South Cheshire College, Dane Bank Avenue, Crewe, Cheshire CW2 8AB

**Derby**
Derby College of Further Education, Wilmorton, Derby DE2 8UG

**Dundee**
Dundee College of Commerce, 30 Constitution Road, Dundee DD3 6TB

**Durham**
New College, Framwellgate Moor, Durham DH1 5ES

**Farnborough**
Farnborough College of Technology, Boundary Road, Farnborough, Hampshire GU14 6SB

**Kettering**
Tresham College, St Mary's Road, Kettering, Northamptonshire NN15 7BS

**Lancaster**
Lancaster and Morecambe College of Further Education, Morecambe Road, Lancaster, Lancashire LA1 2TY

**Leeds**
Park Lane College of Further Education, Park Lane, Leeds LS3 1AA

### Lewes
Lewes Technical College, Mountfield Road, Lewes, East Sussex BN7 2XH

### London
College for the Distributive Trades, 30 Leicester Square, London WC2H 7LE
Paddington College, 25 Paddington Green, London W2 1NB
Southwark College, The Cut, London SE1 8LE

### Loughborough
Loughborough Technical College, Radmoor, Loughborough, Leicestershire LE11 3BT

### Newbury
Newbury College, Oxford Road, Newbury, Berkshire RG13 1PQ

### Nottingham
Broxtowe College of Further Education, High Road, Chilwell, Beeston, Nottingham NG9 4AH

### Portsmouth
Highbury College of Technology, Cosham, Portsmouth, Hampshire PO6 2SA

### Redhill
East Surrey College, Gatton Point, Redhill, Surrey RH1 2JX

### Rotherham
Rockingham College of Further Education, Wath-upon-Dearne, Rotherham, South Yorkshire S63 6PX

### Solihull
Solihull College of Technology, Blossomfield Road, Solihull, West Midlands B91 1SB

### Southport
Southport College of Art and Technology, Mornington Road, Southport, Merseyside PR9 0TT

### St Austell
Mid-Cornwall College of Further Education, Palace Road, St Austell, Cornwall PL25 4BW

### St Helens
St Helens College of Technology, Water Street, St Helens, Merseyside WA10 1PZ

**Stockport**
Stockport College of Technology, Wellington Road South, Stockport, Cheshire SK1 3UQ

**Wallsend**
North Tyneside College of Further Education, Embleton Avenue, Wallsend, Tyne and Wear NE28 9NL

**Welwyn Garden City**
de Havilland College, The Campus, Welwyn Garden City, Hertfordshire AL8 6AH

**Windsor**
Windsor and Maidenhead College, Claremont Road, Windsor, Berkshire SL4 3AZ

**Worthing**
Northbrook College of Design and Technology, Broadwater Road, Worthing, West Sussex BN14 8HJ

## Certificate of Travel Agency Competence (COTAC, Parts 1 and/or 2)

**Aberdeen**
Aberdeen College of Commerce, Holburn Street, Aberdeen AB9 2YT

**Altrincham**
South Trafford College, Manchester Road, West Timperley, Altrincham, Cheshire WA14 5PQ

**Amersham**
Amersham College of Further Education, Art and Design, Stanley Hill, Amersham, Buckinghamshire HP7 9HN

**Carshalton**
Carshalton College of Further Education, Nightingale Road, Carshalton, Surrey SM5 2EJ

**Dundee**
Dundee College of Commerce, 30 Constitution Road, Dundee DD3 6TB

**Durham**
New College, Framwellgate Moor, Durham DH1 5ES

**Glasgow**
Glasgow College of Food Technology, 230 Cathedral Street, Glasgow G1 2TG

**Leeds**
Park Lane College of Further Education, Park Lane, Leeds LS3 1AA

**Nottingham**
Broxtowe College of Further Education, High Road, Chilwell, Beeston, Nottingham NG9 4AH

**Portsmouth**
Highbury College of Technology, Cosham, Portsmouth, Hampshire PO6 2SA

**Solihull**
Solihull College of Technology, Blossomfield Road, Solihull, West Midlands B91 1SB

**Southport**
Southport College of Art and Technology, Mornington Road, Southport, Merseyside PR9 0TT

**Welwyn Garden City**
de Havilland College, The Campus, Welwyn Garden City, Hertfordshire AL8 6AH

**Windsor**
Windsor and Maidenhead College, Claremont Road, Windsor, Berkshire SL4 3AZ

**Worthing**
Northbrook College of Design and Technology, Broadwater Road, Worthing, West Sussex BN14 8HJ

## BTEC (Business and Technician Education Council) or SCOTVEC (Scottish Vocational Education Council) Courses

**Aberdeen**
Aberdeen College of Commerce, Holburn Street, Aberdeen AB9 2YT

**Altrincham**
South Trafford College, Manchester Road, West Timperley, Altrincham, Cheshire WA14 5PQ

**Amersham**
Amersham College of Further Education, Art and Design, Stanley Hill, Amersham, Buckinghamshire HP7 9HN

**Aylesbury**
Aylesbury College of Further Education, Oxford Road, Aylesbury, Buckinghamshire HP21 8PD

**Belfast**
Rupert Stanley College, Tower Street, Belfast BT5 4FH

**Braintree**
Braintree College of Further Education, Church Lane, Braintree, Essex CM7 5SN

**Bristol**
Soundwell Technical College, St Stephens Road, Soundwell, Bristol BS16 4RL

**Bury**
Bury Metropolitan College, Market Street, Bury, Lancashire BL9 0BG

**Buxton**
High Peak College of Further Education, Harpur Hill, Buxton, Derbyshire SK17 9JZ

**Cambridge**
Cambridge College of Further Education, Newmarket Road, Cambridge CB5 8EG

**Cardiff**
South Glamorgan Institute of Higher Education, Colchester Avenue, Cardiff CF3 7XR

**Carlisle**
Carlisle Technical College, Victoria Place, Carlisle, Cumbria CA1 1HS

**Carshalton**
Carshalton College of Further Education, Nightingale Road, Carshalton, Surrey SM5 2EJ

**Coventry**
Henley College of Further Education, Henley Road, Bell Green, Coventry, West Midlands CV2 1ED

**Crewe**
South Cheshire College, Dane Bank Avenue, Crewe, Cheshire CW2 8AB

**Dartford**
North West Kent College of Technology, Miskin Road, Dartford, Kent DA1 2LU

**Derby**
Derby College of Further Education, Wilmorton, Derby DE2 8UG

**Dundee**
Dundee College College of Commerce, 30 Constitution Road, Dundee DD3 6TB

**Durham**
New College, Framwellgate Moor, Durham DH1 5ES

**Folkestone**
South Kent College of Technology, Shorncliffe Road, Folkestone, Kent CT20 2NA

**Glasgow**
Glasgow College of Food Technology, 230 Cathedral Street, Glasgow G1 2TG

**Kettering**
Tresham College, St Mary's Road, Kettering, Northamptonshire NN15 7BS

**King's Lynn**
Norfolk College of Arts and Technology, Tennyson Avenue, King's Lynn, Norfolk PE30 2QW

**Lancaster**
Lancaster and Morecambe College of Further Education, Morecambe Road, Lancaster, Lancashire LA1 2TY

**Leeds**
Park Lane College of Further Education, Park Lane, Leeds LS3 1AA

**Lewes**
Lewes Technical College, Mountfield Road, Lewes, East Sussex
BN7 2XH

**London**
College for the Distributive Trades, 30 Leicester Square, London
WC2H 7LE
Hendon College, The Burroughs, Hendon, London NW4 3DE

**Loughborough**
Loughborough Technical College, Radmoor, Loughborough, Leicestershire LE11 3BT

**Macclesfield**
Macclesfield College of Further Education, Park Lane, Macclesfield, Cheshire SK11 8LF

**Newbury**
Newbury College, Oxford Road, Newbury, Berkshire RG13 1PQ

**Newtonabbey**
Newtonabbey Technical College, Shore Road, Newtonabbey,
County Antrim, Northern Ireland BT37 9RS

**Nottingham**
Broxtowe College of Further Education, High Road, Chilwell,
Beeston, Nottingham NG9 4AH

**Portsmouth**
Highbury College of Technology, Cosham, Portsmouth, Hampshire PO6 2SA

**Redditch**
Redditch College, Redditch, Worcestershire B98 8DW

**Redhill**
East Surrey College, Gatton Point, Redhill, Surrey RH1 2JX

**Rotherham**
Rockingham College of Further Education, Wath-upon-Dearne,
Rotherham, South Yorkshire S63 6PX

**Scunthorpe**
North Lindsey College of Technology, Kingsway, Scunthorpe,
South Humberside DN17 1AJ

**Solihull**
Solihull College of Technology, Blossomfield Road, Solihull, West
Midlands B91 1SB

**Southport**
Southport College of Art and Technology, Mornington Road,
Southport, Merseyside PR9 0TT

**St Austell**
Mid-Cornwall College of Further Education, Palace Road, St
Austell, Cornwall PL25 4BW

**St Helens**
St Helens College of Technology, Water Street, St Helens,
Merseyside WA10 1PZ

**Stockport**
Stockport College of Technology, Wellington Road South, Stockport, Cheshire SK1 3UQ

**Stratford-upon-Avon**
South Warwickshire College of Further Education, The Willows
North, Alcester Road, Stratford-upon-Avon, Warwickshire
CV37 9QR

**Taunton**
Somerset College of Arts and Technology, Wellington Road,
Taunton, Somerset TA1 5AX

**Wallsend**
North Tyneside College of Further Education, Embleton Avenue,
Wallsend, Tyne and Wear NE28 9NL

**Welwyn Garden City**
de Havilland College, The Campus, Welwyn Garden City, Hertfordshire AL8 6AH

**Windsor**
Windsor and Maidenhead College, Claremont Road, Windsor,
Berkshire SL4 3AZ

**Worthing**
Northbrook College of Design and Technology, Broadwater
Road, Worthing, West Sussex BN14 8HJ

# Certificate of Tour Operating Practice

### London
College for the Distributive Trades, 30 Leicester Square, London WC2H 7LE (YTS)
Paddington College, 25 Paddington Green, London W2 1NB

### Redditch
Redditch College, Redditch, Worcestershire B98 8DW

### Worthing
Northbrook College of Design and Technology, Broadwater Road, Worthing, West Sussex BN14 8HJ

# Certificate of Travel Studies

### Altrincham
South Trafford College, Manchester Road, West Timperley, Altrincham, Cheshire WA14 5PQ

### Amersham
Amersham College of Further Education, Art and Design, Stanley Hill, Amersham, Buckinghamshire HP7 9HN

### Aylesbury
Aylesbury College of Further Education, Oxford Road, Aylesbury, Buckinghamshire HP21 8PD

### Belvedere
Erith College of Technology, Tower Road, Belvedere, Kent DA17 6JA

### Braintree
Braintree College of Further Education, Church Lane, Braintree, Essex CM7 5SN

### Carshalton
Carshalton College of Further Education, Nightingale Road, Carshalton, Surrey SM5 2EJ

### Coventry
Henley College of Further Education, Henley Road, Bell Green, Coventry, West Midlands CV2 1ED

**Farnborough**
Farnborough College of Technology, Boundary Road, Farnborough, Hampshire GU14 6SB

**Kettering**
Tresham College, St Mary's Road, Kettering, Northamptonshire NN15 7BS

**Lancaster**
Lancaster and Morecambe College of Further Education, Morecambe Road, Lancaster, Lancashire LA1 2TY

**Lewes**
Lewes Technical College, Mountfield Road, Lewes, East Sussex BN7 2XH

**Loughborough**
Loughborough Technical College, Radmoor, Loughborough, Leicestershire LE11 3BT

**Portsmouth**
Highbury College of Technology, Cosham, Portsmouth, Hampshire PO6 2SA

**Redhill**
East Surrey College, Gatton Point, Redhill, Surrey RH1 2JX

**Solihull**
Solihull College of Technology, Blossomfield Road, Solihull, West Midlands B91 1SB

**Southport**
Southport College of Art and Technology, Mornington Road, Southport, Merseyside PR9 0TT

**Stratford-upon-Avon**
South Warwickshire College of Further Education, The Willows North, Alcester Road, Stratford-upon-Avon, Warwickshire CV37 9QR

**Wallsend**
North Tyneside College of Further Education, Embleton Avenue, Wallsend, Tyne and Wear NE28 9NL

**Welwyn Garden City**
de Havilland College, The Campus, Welwyn Garden City, Hertfordshire AL8 6AH

# Sources of Information

Information may be obtained from many different sources. Listed below are a number of organisations which provide useful information about work within the travel industry, as well as the qualifications which can be obtained.

*Don't forget* – your travel agent is an excellent place to find out addresses of tour operators and travel providers. Browse through the brochures!

### General Information
**Association of British Travel Agents**, National Training Board, Waterloo House, 11–17 Chertsey Road, Woking, Surrey GU21 5AL (please note that ABTA can only reply to career enquiries which are accompanied by a large stamped self-addressed envelope)

**British Hotels, Restaurants and Caterers' Association**
40 Duke Street, London W1M 5HR

**British Incoming Tour Operators' Association**
Premier House, 77 Oxford Street, London W1R 1RB

**British Tourist Authority**
Thames Tower, Black's Road, Hammersmith, London W6 9EL

**English Tourist Board**
Thames Tower, Black's Road, Hammersmith, London W6 9EL

**Guild of Guide Lecturers**
2 Bridge Street (Grandma Lees Restaurant), London SW1A 2JR

**Institute of Travel and Tourism**
113 Victoria Street, St Albans, Hertfordshire AL1 3TJ

**London Visitor and Convention Bureau**
26 Grosvenor Gardens, London SW1W 0DU

**Northern Ireland Tourist Board**
River House, 48 High Street, Belfast BT1 2DS

**Scottish Tourist Board**
23 Ravelston Terrace, Edinburgh EH4 3EU

**Tourism Society**
26 Grosvenor Gardens, London SW1W 0DU

**Wales Tourist Board**
Brunel House, 2 Fitzalan Road, Cardiff CF2 1UY

## Air Travel

**Air Transport Industry Training Association**
125 London Road, High Wycombe, Buckinghamshire HP11 1BT

**Britannia Airways**
Luton Airport, Luton, Bedfordshire LU2 9HD

**British Airports Authority**
Gatwick Airport, Gatwick, West Sussex RH6 0HZ

**British Airways**
PO Box 10, Heathrow Airport, Hounslow, Middlesex TW6 2JA

**British Caledonian Airways**
Caledonia House, Crawley, West Sussex RH10 2XA

**British Midland**
Donnington Hall, Castle Donnington, Derby DE7 2SB

**Civil Aviation Authority**
CAA House, 45-49 Kingsway, London WC2B 6TE

## Coach Travel

**National Bus Company**
172 Buckingham Palace Road, London SW1 9TN

**Scottish Bus Group Ltd**
Carron House, 114 George Street, Edinburgh EH2 4LH

**The Bus and Coach Council**
Sardinia House, 52 Lincoln's Inn Fields, London WC2A 3LZ

Also contact individual tour-operating companies and coach operators. You can do this by checking Yellow Pages and the brochures in travel agencies.

## Merchant Navy

**General Council of British Shipping**
30-32 St Mary Axe, London EC3 8ET

## Ferry Services

**Brittany Ferries**
The Brittany Centre, Wharf Road, Portsmouth PO2 8RU

**Caledonian MacBrayne Ferries**
The Ferry Terminal, Gourock, Renfrewshire, Scotland

**Cunard Cruise Services**
South Western House, Canute Road, Southampton SO19 13A

**Hoverspeed**
Western Docks, Dover, Kent

**Thoresen Car Ferries Ltd**
Viking House, Wharf Road, Portsmouth PO2 8TA

**P & O Cruises Ltd**
Duke's Keep, Marsh Lane, Southampton SO9 4GU

**Sally Line**
81 Piccadilly, London W1V 9HF

**Sealink UK Ltd**
Eversholt House, 163–203 Eversholt Street, London NW1 1BG

Other addresses can be found in the *ABC Shipping Guide*.

## Rail Travel

**British Railways Board**
Rail House, PO Box 100, Euston Square, London NW1 2DZ

## Examining Boards

**Business and Technician Education Council (BTEC)**
Central House, Upper Woburn Place, London WC1H 0HH

**Scottish Vocational Education Council (SCOTVEC)**
22 Great King Street, Edinburgh EH3 6QH

**City and Guilds of London Institute (CGLI)**
76 Portland Place, London W1N 4AA

# Further Reading

Many of the following directories and books on careers in travel and tourism are available for reference in school libraries, careers service libraries, and the public libraries.

### Directories
*Directory of Further Education* (for details of courses), CRAC
*Directory of Jobs and Careers Abroad*, Vacation Work
*Further Education in Scotland – Directory of Day Courses*, Scottish Education Department
*Handbook of Tourism and Leisure*, CRAC (includes lists of courses)
*International Directory of Voluntary Work*, Vacation Work
*Job Outlines* (individual leaflets on subjects of travel and tourism, driving, and working in airports, published by COIC and available in most schools and careers offices)
*Occupations*, COIC (contains articles on travel and tourism)
*Summer Employment Directory of the USA*, Vacation Work
*Summer Jobs Abroad*, Vacation Work
*Summer Jobs in Britain*, Vacation Work
*Working Holiday*, Central Bureau for Educational Visits and Exchanges
*Work Your Way Around The World*, Vacation Work

### Specific Areas
*Careers at Sea*, Kogan Page; *Careers in Aviation*, Kogan Page; *Careers in Catering and Hotel Management*, Kogan Page; *Careers in the Holiday Industry*, Kogan Page; *Jobs in Airports*, Kogan Page; *Jobs in Hotels*, Kogan Page; *Working as Aircrew*, Batsford; *Working at an Airport*, Wayland; *Working in Airports*, COIC; *Working in the Travel Business*, Batsford; *Working with British Rail*, Batsford; *Working in Tourism*, COIC; *Working in Travel*, COIC.

### Trade Magazines
*Travel News; Travel Trade Gazette*

(These magazines can be found in the reference section of most public libraries. Also check local newsagents – there are many more general travel magazines on sale to the public.)